Development of a Probabilistic Assessment Methodology for Evaluation of Carbon Dioxide Storage

By Robert C. Burruss, Sean T. Brennan, Philip A. Freeman, Matthew D. Merrill, Leslie F. Ruppert, Mark F. Becker, William N. Herkelrath, Yousif K. Kharaka, Christopher E. Neuzil, Sharon M. Swanson, Troy A. Cook, Timothy R. Klett, Philip H. Nelson, and Christopher J. Schenk

Open-File Report 2009–1035

U.S. Department of the Interior
U.S. Geological Survey

U.S. Department of the Interior
KEN SALAZAR, Secretary

U.S. Geological Survey
Suzette M. Kimball, Acting Director

U.S. Geological Survey, Reston, Virginia: 2009

For product and ordering information:
World Wide Web: *http://www.usgs.gov/pubprod*
Telephone: 1-888-ASK-USGS

For more information on the USGS—the Federal source for science about the Earth,
its natural and living resources, natural hazards, and the environment:
World Wide Web: *http://www.usgs.gov*
Telephone: 1-888-ASK-USGS

Suggested citation:
Burruss, R.C., Brennan, S.T., Freeman, P.A., Merrill, M.D., Ruppert, L.F., Becker, M.F., Herkelrath, W.N., Kharaka, Y.K., Neuzil, C.E., Swanson, S.M., Cook, T.A., Klett, T.R., Nelson, P.H., and Schenk, C.J., 2009, Development of a probabilistic assessment methodology for evaluation of carbon dioxide storage: U.S. Geological Survey Open-File Report 2009–1035, 81 p., available only online at *http://pubs.usgs.gov/of/2009/1035/*.

Contents

Figures

Tables

Conversion Factors

Multiply	By	To obtain
Length		
inch (in.)	2.54	centimeter (cm)
foot (ft)	0.3048	meter (m)
mile (mi)	1.609	kilometer (km)
meter (m)	3.281	foot (ft)
kilometer (km)	0.6214	mile (mi)
Area		
square inch (in^2)	6.452	square centimeter (cm^2)
square foot (ft^2)	0.09290	square meter (m^2)
acre	0.4047	hectare (ha)
acre	0.004047	square kilometer (km^2)
square meter (m^2)	0.0002471	acre
Volume		
gallon (gal)	3.785	liter (L)

Multiply	By	To obtain
barrel (bbl), (petroleum, 1 barrel=42 gal)	0.1590	cubic meter (m^3)
cubic foot (ft^3)	0.02832	cubic meter (m^3)
1,000 cubic feet (MCF)	28.32	cubic meter (m^3)
liter (L)	0.2642	gallon (gal)
cubic meter (m^3)	6.290	barrel (petroleum, 1 barrel = 42 gal)
Mass		
pound, avoirdupois (lb)	0.4536	kilogram (kg)
ton, short (2,000 lb)	0.9072	megagram (Mg)
ton, long (2,240 lb)	1.016	megagram (Mg)
milligram (mg)	0.00003527	ounce, avoirdupois (oz)
gram (g)	0.03527	ounce, avoirdupois (oz)
kilogram (kg)	2.205	pound avoirdupois (lb)
megagram (Mg) = 1 metric ton (t) (1,000 kg)	1.102	ton, short (2,000 lb)
megagram (Mg)	0.9842	ton, long (2,240 lb)
million metric tons	1.102	million short tons
Pressure		
atmosphere, standard (atm)	101.3	kilopascal (kPa)
bar	100	kilopascal (kPa)
pound-force per square inch (lbf/in^2 or psi)	6.895	kilopascal (kPa)
kilopascal (kPa)	0.009869	atmosphere, standard (atm)
kilopascal (kPa)	0.01	bar
kilopascal (kPa)	0.2961	inch of mercury at 60°F (in Hg)
kilopascal (kPa)	0.1450	pound-force per square inch (lbf/in^2)
megapascal (MPa)	145	pound-force per square inch (lbf/in^2)
Pressure gradient		
pound-force per square inch per foot (lb/in^2/ft or psi/ft)	22.62	kilopascal per meter (kPa/m)
Density		
pound per cubic foot (lb/ft^3)	16.02	kilogram per cubic meter (kg/m^3)
pound per cubic foot (lb/ft^3)	0.01602	gram per cubic centimeter (g/cm^3)
kilogram per cubic meter (kg/m^3)	0.06242	pound per cubic foot (lb/ft^3)
gram per cubic centimeter (g/cm^3)	62.4220	pound per cubic foot (lb/ft^3)
Electric power		
megawatt electrical (MWe)	3,600,000,000	joule per hour (J/hr)
Hydraulic conductivity		
meters per second (m/s)	3.281	foot per second (ft/s)
Hydraulic diffusivity		

Multiply	By	To obtain
square meter per second (m^2/s)	10.76	square foot per second (ft^2/s)

Temperature in degrees Celsius (°C) may be converted to degrees Fahrenheit (°F) as follows:
°F=(1.8×°C)+32
Temperature in degrees Fahrenheit (°F) may be converted to degrees Celsius (°C) as follows:
°C=(°F−32)/1.8
Concentrations of chemical constituents in water are given in milligrams per liter (mg/L).

Abbreviations, Acronyms, and Symbols

AU	assessment unit
bbl	petroleum barrel or barrels
BOE	barrel of oil equivalent; see glossary
C	condensate
CCS	carbon capture and storage
C_{EOR}	storage efficiency, conventional enhanced oil recovery
cf/bbl	cubic feet per barrel
C_{F1}	conversion factor, petroleum barrels (42 gallons) to cubic meters: 0.159 bbl/m^3
C_{F2}	conversion factor, acre-feet to cubic meters: 1,233.5 m^3/acre-ft
C_G	growth factor
CH_4	methane
CO_2	carbon dioxide
C_{SE}	storage efficiency factor
CV_{OC}	cumulative volume of oil accumulations and condensate
C_{WD}	correction factor, water recharge or water flooding
D	depth
DOE	U.S. Department of Energy
EOR	enhanced oil recovery
EPA	U.S. Environmental Protection Agency
FVF	formation volume factor
GIS	geographic information system
GOR	gas:oil ratio
H_2O	water
I_R	incremental recovery
MCF	thousand cubic feet
MMbbl	million barrels
MMBOE	million barrels of oil equivalent
MMCF	millions of cubic feet
Mt	million metric tons
NCV	net cumulative volume
NOGA	USGS National Oil and Gas Assessment
N_{TP}	fraction of storage interval thickness with porosity greater than the minimum used for evaluation of petroleum resources (fraction)
O	oil
OOIP	original oil in place
P	pressure

psi	pounds per square inch
PT	physical trap
PT_D	physical trap, discovered
PT_{DS}	physical traps, discovered
PT_S	physical traps
PT_U	physical trap, undiscovered
PT_{US}	physical traps, undiscovered
PVT	pressure, volume, temperature
R_F	oil recovery factor
s	second
SAU	storage assessment unit
SAUs	storage assessment units
S_{EOR}	storage, conventional enhanced oil recovery
SF	saline formation
S_{NCV}	storage, net cumulative volume
S_{TKV}	storage, total known volume
S_{TTV}	storage, total trap volume
T_A	trap area
TDS	total dissolved solids
T_I	thickness, interval
TKV	total known volume
TTV	total trap volume
USGS	U.S. Geological Survey
ρ_{CO2}	density of carbon dioxide
Φ	porosity

Development of a Probabilistic Assessment Methodology for Evaluation of Carbon Dioxide Storage

By Robert C. Burruss, Sean T. Brennan, Philip A. Freeman, Matthew D. Merrill, Leslie F. Ruppert, Mark F. Becker, William N. Herkelrath, Yousif K. Kharaka, Christopher E. Neuzil, Sharon M. Swanson, Troy A. Cook, Timothy R. Klett, Philip H. Nelson, and Christopher J. Schenk

1. Introduction

1.1. Purpose and Scope

The U.S. Geological Survey (USGS) has a long history of assessing national and global ground- and surface-water resources and geologically based energy and mineral resources. In 2007, the Energy Independence and Security Act (Public Law 110–140) authorized the USGS to conduct a national assessment of geologic storage resources for carbon dioxide (CO_2) in cooperation with the U.S. Environmental Protection Agency (EPA) and the U.S. Department of Energy (DOE). A first step in planning for a national assessment is the development of a methodology to estimate storage resource potential that can be applied uniformly to geologic formations across the United States.

This report defines and describes an assessment methodology for evaluation of the resource potential for storage of CO_2 in the subsurface. Descriptions of assessment methods are available in the literature that address storage resources and capacities at a variety of scales, using a variety of storage mechanisms (Bachu and others, 2007; Bradshaw and others, 2007; U.S. Department of Energy, National Energy Technology Laboratory, 2008a). The methodology presented in this report is intended for evaluations from the regional to subregional scale in which storage assessment units (SAUs) can be defined on the basis of common geologic and hydrologic characteristics. The resource that is assessed is the volume of pore space into which CO_2 can be injected and retained for tens of thousands of years. The calculation of subsurface pore volume for potential CO_2 storage has been described in a number of publications (Bachu, 2003: Bradshaw, 2004; Bachu and others, 2007; U.S. Department of Energy, National Energy Technology Laboratory, 2008a; van der Meer and Egberts, 2008). The methodology in this report uses probabilistic methods to incorporate uncertainty and natural variability in volumetric parameters. The methodology incorporates statistical evaluation of the sizes and numbers of potential storage sites to identify the range of possible storage resources within a storage assessment unit and the probability that some fraction of all the storage sites could retain a minimum storage mass of CO_2. The estimated mass of storage resource is further evaluated with parameters that describe the probability of successful containment of CO_2.

As discussed below, the physical properties of CO_2 at subsurface pressures and temperatures are similar to the properties of petroleum. Therefore, the CO_2 resource assessment methods are built on the principles of USGS geologic oil and gas resource evaluation and assessment that were most recently described in Charpentier and Klett (2005), Crovelli (2005), Klett and Schmoker (2005), Klett and others (2005a), Schmoker (2005), and Schmoker and Klett (2005). These methods have been developed and refined over the last 40 years through periodically updated USGS national oil and gas assessments (NOGA) and world energy assessments. The current NOGA methodology is a refinement of methods that were extensively peer reviewed (Buckley and others, 1999; Curtis and others, 2001). NOGA reports on methodology and projects are recognized as the only publicly available, comprehensive assessment of U.S. oil and gas resources. NOGA data are used widely by policymakers, including the U.S. Congress, other Federal agencies, State geological surveys and oil and gas commissions, Tribal governments, and local governments, and by landowners, industry, and researchers.

Oil and gas assessments conducted by the USGS evaluate the technically recoverable, undiscovered resource, which is a fraction of the total in-place resource that may be recoverable with technology available at the time of the assessment and for some limited time into the future, for example, on the order of decades. Similarly, this assessment methodology for CO_2 storage resources focuses on the technically accessible resource, not a total in-place resource volume. This is a resource that may be available using present-day geological and engineering knowledge and technology for CO_2 injection into geologic formations. However, no economic factors are used in the estimation of the volume of the resource.

The methodology emphasizes large storage masses of CO_2 for two reasons. First, petroleum resource assessment research indicates that most of the resource volume is found in a relatively small number (up to a few tens) of large accumulations, despite the possible presence of many (possibly hundreds) of much smaller accumulations. Second, successful deployment of geologic storage as one of many carbon management technologies to mitigate climate change will require storage of large masses of CO_2 (hundreds of millions to thousands of millions of metric tons) as discussed in Pacala and Socolow (2004) and Brennan and Burruss (2006). Therefore, we need assessment methods that can identify the storage assessment units (SAUs) that have the potential to store the largest masses of CO_2 and thereby have significance for national policy discussions on implementation of geologic sequestration technologies. However, the methods described here can be applied to storage resources of any size and are applicable to smaller areas than those required for the national assessment.

The present stage of development of the methodology focuses on storage resources in porous geologic formations in sedimentary basins. In particular, the methodology addresses the storage resources of SAUs that contain physical traps (PTs) that have produced petroleum, traps that contain petroleum but have not been discovered, and parts of formations between traps that are filled with saline formation water, called saline formations (SF) in this report. Formations that have never produced oil and gas can also be evaluated with this methodology. Storage in other types of geological formations, such as unminable coal beds, organic-matter-rich shale, basalt, or other potential geologic storage formations, is not addressed at this time. However, the probabilistic methods used in this report should be flexible enough that they can be modified to evaluate other types of geologic storage resources for CO_2 sequestration.

This report is intended for a technical audience of geologists and engineers who are familiar with the concepts of petroleum geology, natural resource assessment, and CO_2 sequestration science. Following publication of this report, the USGS will establish a panel of experts in CO_2 sequestration science from Federal and State agencies, academia, industry, and international geoscience agencies to review the methodology before it is published in the Federal Register, as required by the Energy Independence and Security Act of 2007 (Public Law 110–140). After review, an executive summary may be written for a nontechnical audience.

1.2. Conceptual Framework

Probabilistic methods of natural resource assessment are built on models of resource formation (mineral deposit models, petroleum systems) and models of resource discovery (discovery process or deposit simulation models). Developing geologically consistent models for the formation of deposits of a geologic commodity (for example, gold, petroleum, copper) is a critical step in the resource assessment process. The models provide a basis for understanding how high concentrations of a commodity (a deposit or accumulation) form in the earth. This knowledge improves evaluations of the possible distribution of resource accumulations in unexplored areas. Discovery process or deposit simulation models are developed from the history of exploration and discovery of resource accumulations. Statistical models based on the size and number of accumulations discovered over time are used to estimate distributions of the size and number of undiscovered accumulations. In areas with resource potential but little or no history of exploration and deposit discovery, deposit models based on geologic analogs of extensively explored areas can be used to estimate resource potential (Klett and others, 2000; Schmoker and Klett, 2000).

For geologic sequestration of CO_2 to be a successful technology for limiting CO_2 emissions to the atmosphere, a geologic resource must be identified that can retain (trap) CO_2 in the subsurface. The retention time must be long, thousands to hundreds of thousands of years, to prevent CO_2 from returning to the atmosphere or migrating in ways that may cause adverse environmental effects such as contamination of shallow ground water. Therefore, the resource for geologic storage of CO_2 must have two properties: space ("porosity," pore volume, or pore space) in which to inject CO_2 and a trapping mechanism that will retain the CO_2 in that space. Any area in the crust of the Earth that has a relatively high concentration of both pore space and trapping mechanisms can be considered an "accumulation" of the storage resource. Another geologic property of the subsurface that affects our concepts of the resource for CO_2 storage is that there is no "empty" pore space in which to inject CO_2. All pore space is filled with a fluid, such as formation water, crude oil, or gas. Therefore, injection of CO_2 will cause the CO_2 to interact with the existing pore-filling fluid or the pore walls in several ways, physically displacing the fluid or dissolving and mixing with the fluids or reacting with the pore walls.

CO_2 at subsurface conditions has a lower density than formation water (fig. 1) so that CO_2 injected into subsurface pore space will displace formation water and rise buoyantly until it encounters a permeability barrier. At subsurface temperatures and pressures, CO_2 is a fluid with a density that is within the range of densities of naturally occurring crude oil and significantly higher than the density of natural gas (fig. 1).

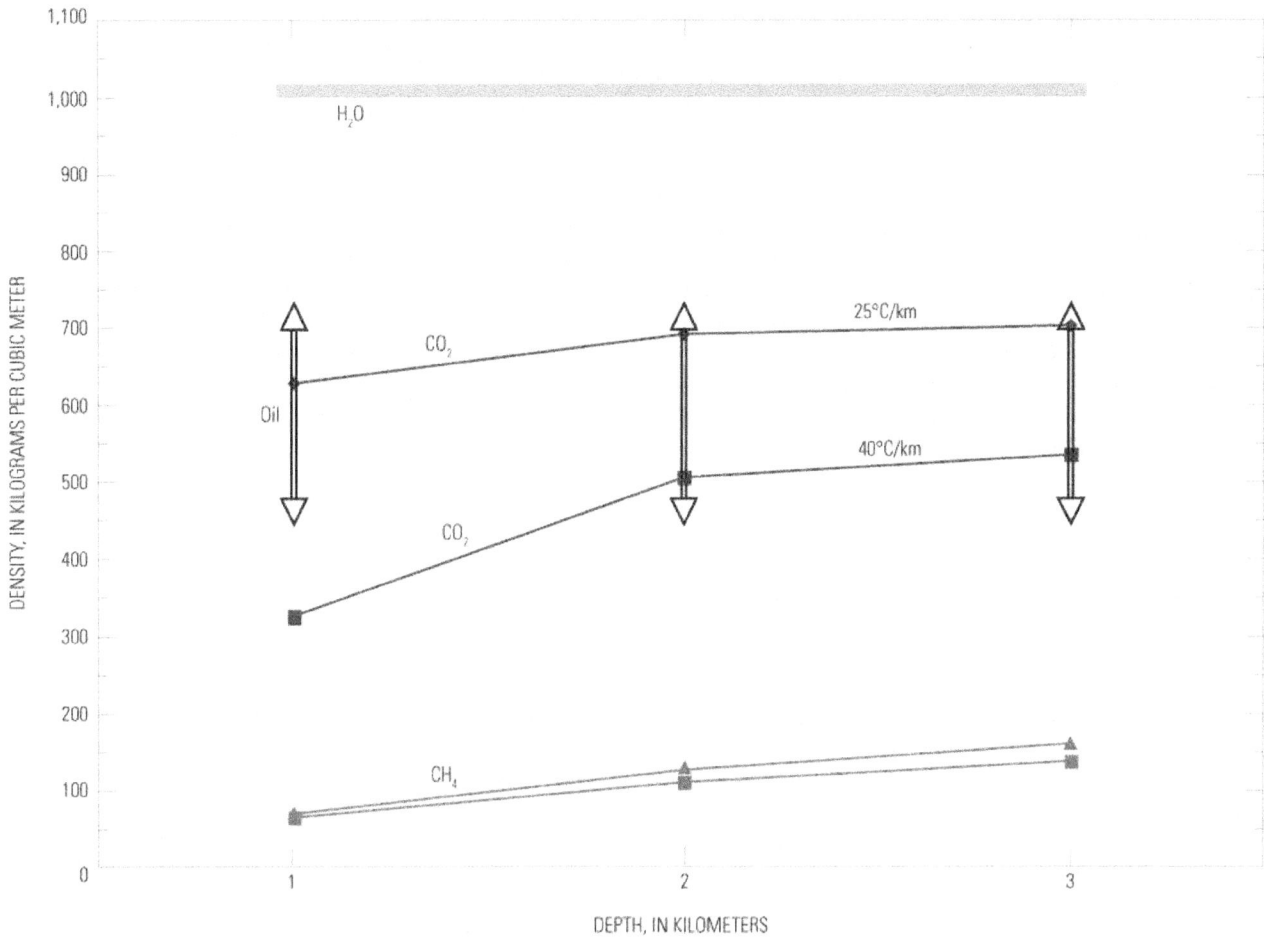

Figure 1. Densities of CO_2 (carbon dioxide) and CH_4 (methane, the main component of natural gas) at depths of 1, 2, and 3 kilometers (km) at two different thermal gradients: 25°C/km and 40°C/km. The ranges of values for formation water (H_2O) and crude oil are shown for comparison.

In the subsurface, the density and buoyancy of CO_2 are similar to those of crude oils so that a free CO_2 phase will flow and accumulate in ways that are directly analogous to the flow and accumulation of oil and gas in traps. The key features of petroleum accumulations (petroleum systems, see figure 2 and discussion below) are adequate pore volume to contain the fluid, a three-dimensional trap with a seal (permeability barrier) to retain the fluid, and adequate permeability (flow properties) to allow extraction of fluid by flow to a wellbore. Because of the similarities in properties between CO_2 and petroleum in the subsurface, resource assessment methods based on petroleum system models and discovery process models appear to be logical starting points for development of methods to assess the storage resource for CO_2 sequestration.

The geologic commodity that is assessed in this methodology is pore space in the subsurface. The fraction of the total volume of pore space within a storage assessment unit (SAU) that could be occupied by

CO_2 can be described as the total in-place resource. The methodology presented in this report addresses that fraction of the total resource that is technically accessible with present-day knowledge and experience. The only parts of a storage formation with documented pore volume and trap geometry that can retain a buoyant fluid and that have measured flow properties are the known petroleum accumulations. The data used to estimate pore volume in these accumulations can be used directly, along with the known accumulation size and number distributions, to estimate storage resource in PTs. Furthermore, the data can be extrapolated to estimate storage resource in SFs. Statistical evaluation of the distributions of the geologic properties that control the volume of pore space and the distribution of the size and number of traps combine to serve as the basis of the methods in this report.

1.3. Organization of the Report

The report is divided into five sections. Section 1 is a review of the conceptual framework for assessment of storage resources used in this report. Section 2 describes the geologic model on which the methodology is based and the factors that may have the greatest effect on storage resources. Section 2 also includes descriptions of the geologic concepts of CO_2 storage in SFs and in oil and gas reservoirs, or PTs. Section 3 introduces the description of the volumetric equations, Monte Carlo simulation techniques, and the necessary input data to estimate storage resources in depleted oil and gas reservoirs (PTs) and SFs (SF) that occur within the same strata as the oil and gas reservoirs. Prototype data input forms for each type of storage are included in appendix A and are described in section 3. Section 3 also includes data sources, data quality, and examples of storage sizes generated by the methodology. A discussion of the data gaps, knowledge gaps, and research directions needed to (1) reduce the uncertainties in estimates of CO_2 storage resources and (2) refine the statistical modeling of geological storage resource estimates is included in section 4. Conclusions are presented in section 5. A glossary follows the "References Cited."

2. Geologic Concepts and Models for Probabilistic Assessment of CO_2 Storage Resources

2.1. Assessment Units

2.1.1. Geologic Concept: Physical Trap and Saline Formation Components

The definition of a storage assessment unit (SAU) requires a geologic concept for CO_2 storage. The fundamental storage process described in the conceptual framework for this assessment methodology is retention within geologic formations by permeability barriers. The SAU is a mappable rock package that consists of a porous flow unit for storage that is bounded by a sealing formation (permeability barrier, cap rock, or confining layer). Within the SAU there are two geologic components: the physical traps (PTs), which are three-dimensional containers, and the saline formation (SF), which is the porous flow unit between PTs. The SF is referred to as the "saline aquifer" in some sequestration literature. The objective of the methodology is to quantify the storage resource within PTs and that portion of the SF that will retain buoyant CO_2. The trapping mechanisms other than physical trapping that may operate in the SF are described below.

The components of a petroleum system that are most directly analogous to CO_2 storage are petroleum migration and accumulation, which are schematically illustrated in figure 2. In this illustration, oil and gas are generated at some depth greater than the reservoir rock and migrate into the reservoir along a fault.

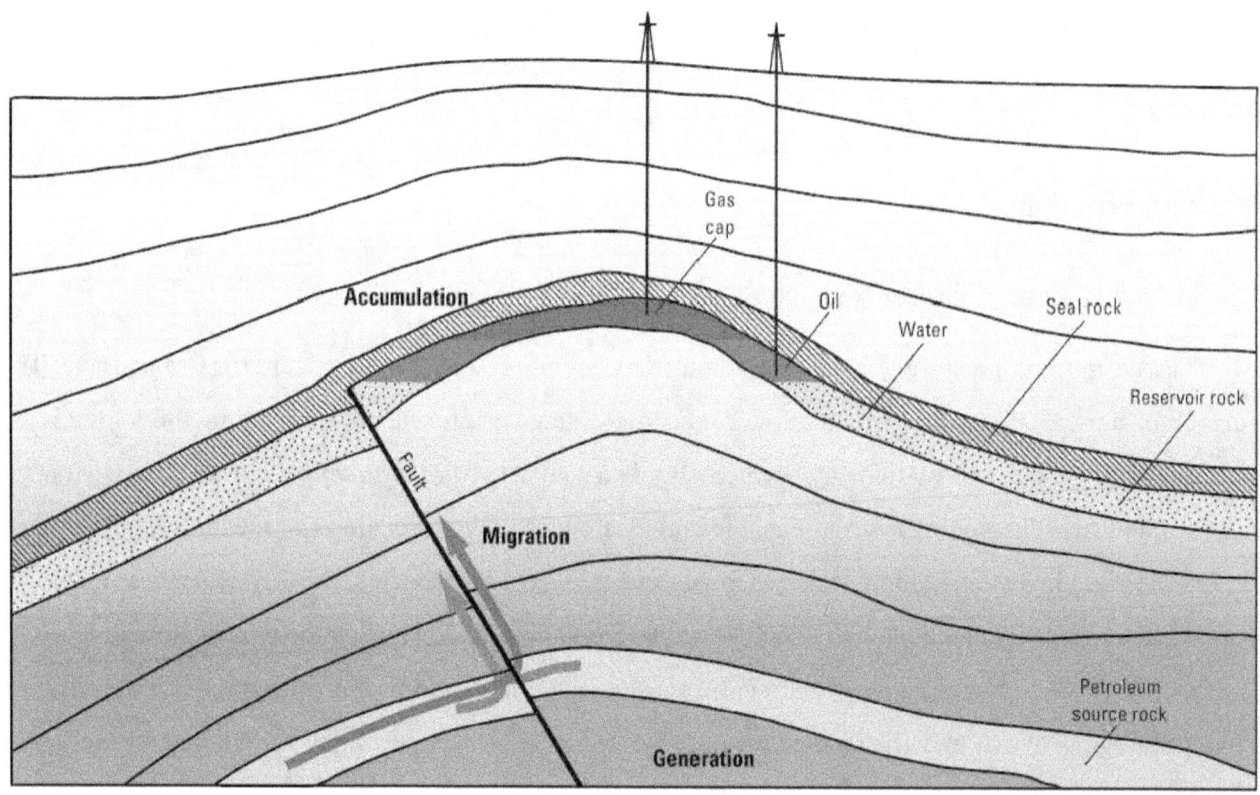

Figure 2. Schematic diagram of petroleum generation, migration, and accumulation. Redrawn from a copyrighted diagram by ExxonMobil presented by the American Geological Institute in the Earth Science World Image Bank (as image h5inrc) at *http://www.earthscienceworld.org/images/index.html*, used with permission.

When the buoyant hydrocarbons encounter a porous and permeable reservoir unit, the hydrocarbons displace formation water and migrate updip beneath a seal. When the hydrocarbons encounter a trap enclosed by the seal, the buoyant fluids continue to displace formation water, forming an accumulation. During geologic sequestration of CO_2, the buoyant fluid is injected into the storage formation (one component of the SAU) from a wellbore. However, as shown in figure 1, the CO_2 density is less than that of formation water and commonly falls in the range of densities of crude oils. Therefore, CO_2 will migrate and accumulate in a trap enclosed by a seal in the same way that petroleum accumulates.

The PTs can either be discovered traps (PT_Ds), by definition the traps that were discovered during oil and gas exploration, or undiscovered traps (PT_Us). The PT_Ds described here are defined only as the PTs that have produced oil and gas, excluding any traps that may have been discovered but that have not produced any volume of hydrocarbons or water. The potential storage volumes of the PT_Ds are based on rock and fluid properties and volumes measured during petroleum exploration and production. Potential storage volumes in the PT_Us can be inferred from the volumes of technically recoverable, undiscovered oil and gas evaluated

8

during the USGS National Oil and Gas Assessment (NOGA). The volumetric properties of the SF are estimated from the properties measured in the PT_Ds and in wildcat (nonproducing) exploration boreholes.

The total storage resource within an SAU is the sum of the resource volumes in the PTs and SF. A schematic illustration of the relationships of PTs and SF in an SAU is shown in figure 3. This model for the SAU is also called the "fill and spill model" for CO_2 storage. In the cross section of an SAU illustrated in figure 3, there are segments that are classified as PT_Ds that are larger than the minimum size (PT_D1 and PT_D3) and a segment that is a small discovered trap (PT_D2) that did not contain commercial volumes of petroleum. Therefore, the potential storage resource in PT_D2 is included in the resource within the SF part of the SAU.

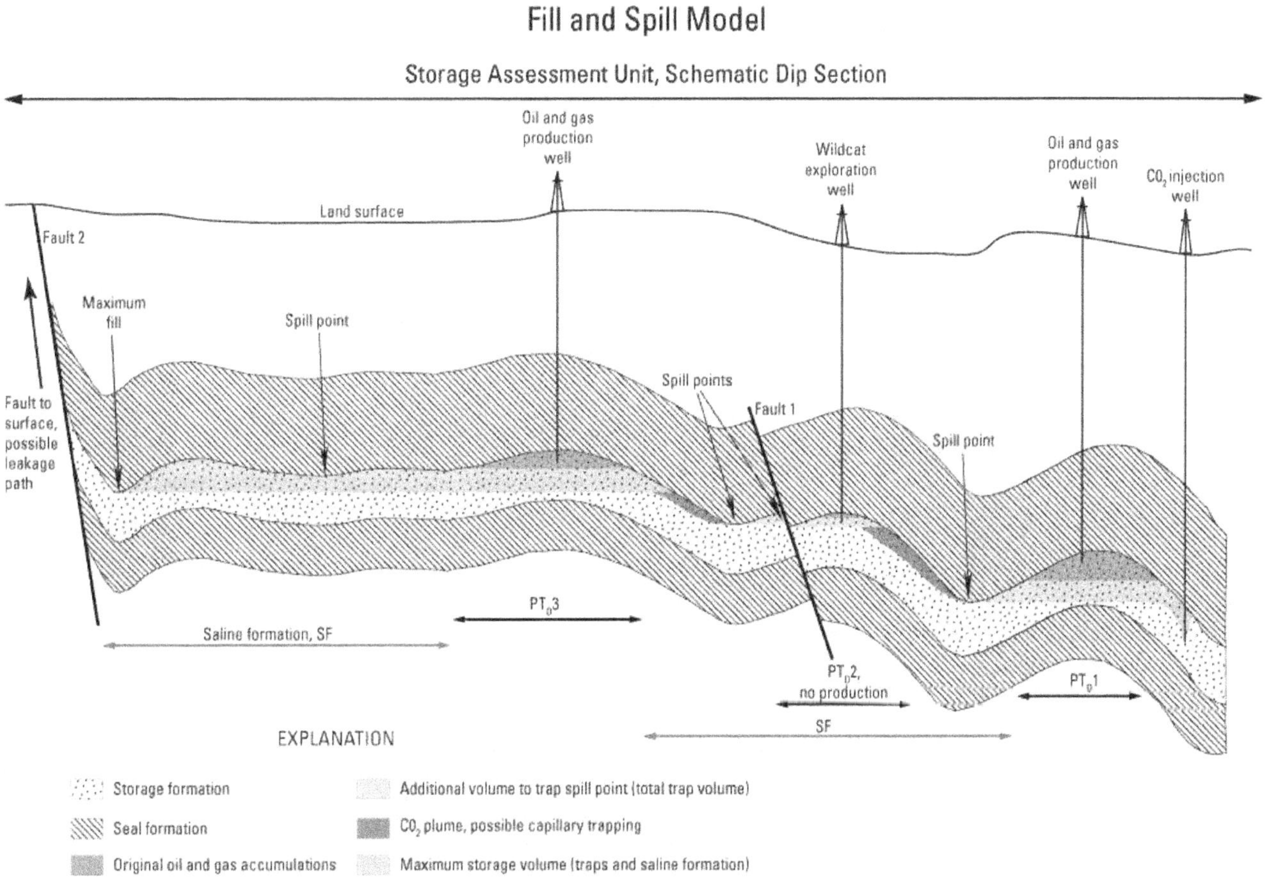

Fill and Spill Model

Storage Assessment Unit, Schematic Dip Section

Figure 3. A schematic cross section through a storage assessment unit (SAU) illustrating the relationship between discovered physical traps (PT_Ds) and the saline formation (SF) in a fill and spill model.

The relationships between the storage resources in the PTs and the SF of this hypothetical SAU can be illustrated by considering the filling sequence of PTs and SF as CO_2 is injected in the downdip leg of PT_D1. The initially injected CO_2 should flow buoyantly into PT_D1, filling the volume of storage resource that can be estimated from the cumulative production of hydrocarbons. Continued injection will fill the additional volume of the trap to the spill point, at which point it will continue to flow updip into PT_D2. PT_D2 had hydrocarbon shows in the wildcat exploration well but did not contain commercial volumes of hydrocarbons. Therefore, there are no production data to evaluate this PT_D. Continued injection will fill the trap to the spill point on fault 1, shown as a laterally transmissive fault in figure 3. Once a small trap on the footwall of the fault is filled, additional injected CO_2 will spill into PT_D3. All of the storage resource within the formation between PT_D1 and PT_D3 is in the SF. The storage resource of PT_D3 is estimated from the cumulative volume of hydrocarbon production from this trap. If the amount of injected CO_2 exceeds the volume of PT_D3, it will migrate laterally under the seal, and the additional CO_2 will accumulate until it reaches a regional spill point. It may be possible to store additional volumes of CO_2 until the total injected volume reaches another regional spill point labeled "maximum fill." This could be the maximum amount of technically accessible storage resource because as shown in figure 3, fault 2 extends to the surface. If the fault surface is permeable, then it could be a leakage pathway to the surface if CO_2 injection continued until CO_2 spilled updip to the fault.

In this schematic illustration, the only parts of the SAU along the cross section that have measured volumetric and flow parameters are within PT_D1 and PT_D3. Limited amounts of data may be available from wildcat wells and small PT_DS (such as PT_D2), but the properties of the SF must be inferred from the properties documented in PT_D1 and PT_D3.

2.1.2. Extent

The vertical extent of an SAU in depth is determined by the pressure, volume, and temperature (PVT) properties of CO_2, whereas the area of the SAU is defined by the geology. The phase relations of CO_2 are shown in figure 4. The critical point of CO_2 is the maximum temperature and pressure at which liquid and vapor CO_2 can coexist (fig. 4).

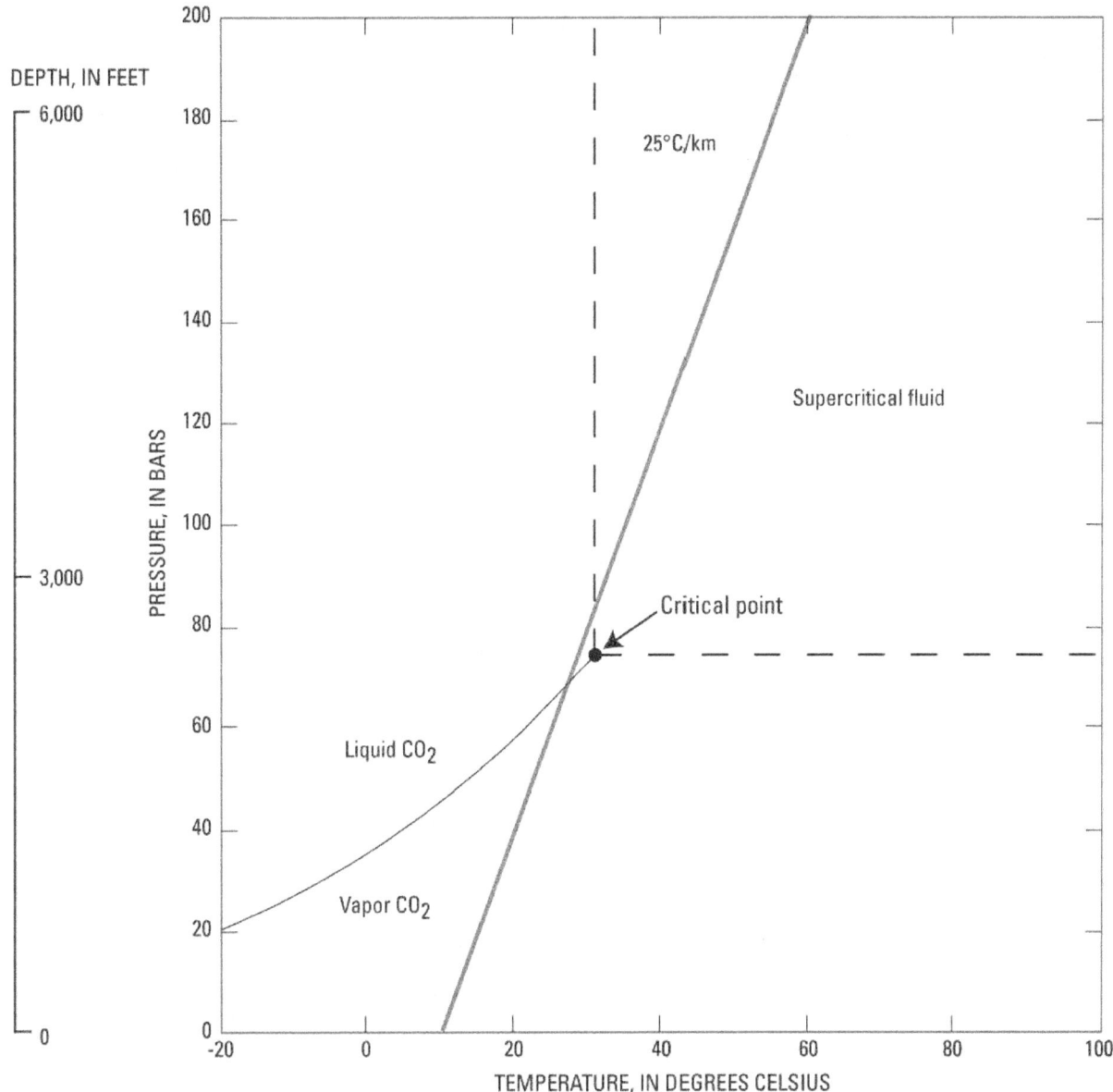

Figure 4. Pressure-temperature diagram of the phase behavior of CO_2 showing the liquid-vapor coexistence curve terminating in the critical point. At pressures and temperatures higher than this point, CO_2 is a fluid with variable density commonly referred to as a supercritical fluid. The vertical bar to the left of the pressure axis shows the approximate depth in feet for a hydrostatic pressure gradient. The red line labeled 25°C/km shows the pressures and temperatures in the subsurface for this thermal gradient and a hydrostatic pressure gradient. Note that at depths greater than 3,000 ft, CO_2 should be supercritical in the subsurface.

At temperatures and pressures greater than the critical point, CO_2 is supercritical and has densities in the range of 500 to 700 kilograms per cubic meter (kg/m^3). The pressure and temperature requirements are typically met at depths greater than 800 meters (m, or about 2,600 feet) at hydrostatic pressure conditions. To limit the potential of CO_2 migrating to pressure and temperature conditions where it could convert from the supercritical state to liquid and vapor, we have chosen a minimum depth of storage of 3,000 feet (ft). Although CO_2 can be stored at depths of less than 3,000 ft, the amount of storage per unit volume of pore space may be significantly less than that at depths greater than 3,000 ft, particularly if CO_2 is in the vapor phase. Therefore, the potential for additions to the storage resource may be relatively small. The minimum depth of storage sets the upper depth limit of the SAU, which in turn limits the areal extent of the SAU on the updip portions of the SAU.

A lower depth limit for CO_2 storage is more arbitrary than the upper depth limit, and at least one methodology (U.S. Department of Energy, National Energy Technology Laboratory, 2008a) does not set any depth limit. However, CO_2 injected at the wellhead within the range of pipeline pressures, for example, 150 bar (2,175 pounds per square inch, psi), results in pressures at the bottom of the well that will be equal to or higher than hydrostatic pressure at depths of 1 to 3 km as shown in figure 5. Therefore, CO_2 injected at these depths will displace normally pressured formation water without additional compression. If injection wellhead pressure from the delivery pipeline is slightly higher than illustrated in this figure, injection depths without additional compression can extend to about 13,000 ft (~4 km). Therefore, we have chosen to limit the maximum depth of assessed units to 13,000 ft. If geologic and hydrologic conditions indicate that CO_2 storage may be possible at greater depths, then this storage can be assessed and reported as potential additions to the CO_2 storage estimates. The process and consequences of the creation of the SAU are shown in an example using the Frio Formation in figure 6.

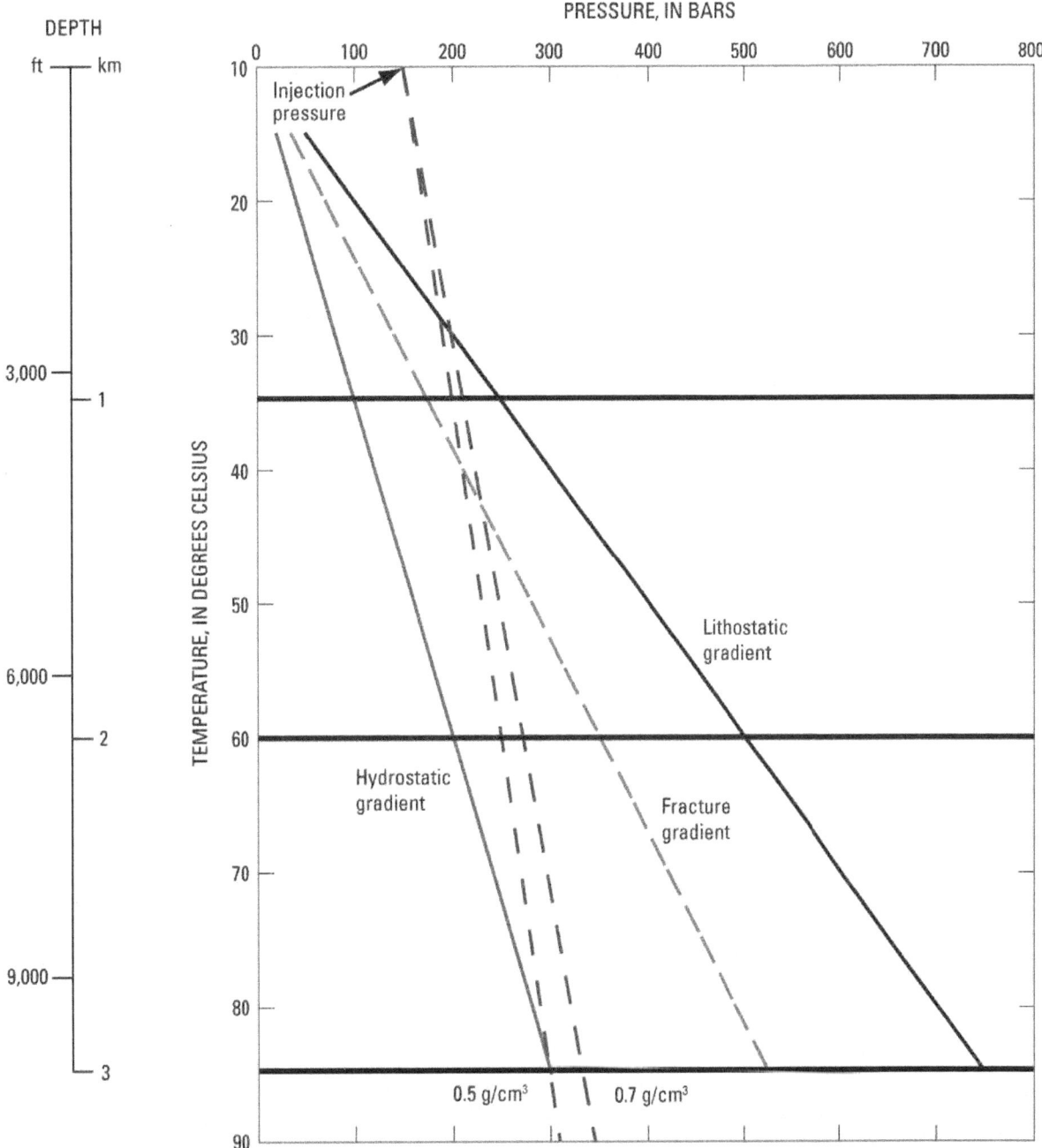

Figure 5. Approximate pressure versus depth relationships for CO_2 at two different densities compared to subsurface pressure in a hydrostatic column of formation water (hydrostatic gradient), pressure due to the load of the rock column (lithostatic gradient), and a generic gradient for the pressure necessary to fracture the rock (fracture gradient). The dashed blue lines show the approximate change in pressure with depth for a static column of CO_2 extending from the top of an injection well (injection pressure) into the subsurface for CO_2 at two different densities. The densities are 0.5 and 0.7 grams per cubic centimeter (g/cm^3). The straight lines are an approximation of the pressure versus depth relationship, which will be curved and a function of injection pressure, injection rate, and other flow variables. The pressure labeled "Injection pressure" is in the range of pressures in CO_2 pipelines for enhanced-oil-recovery (EOR) projects.

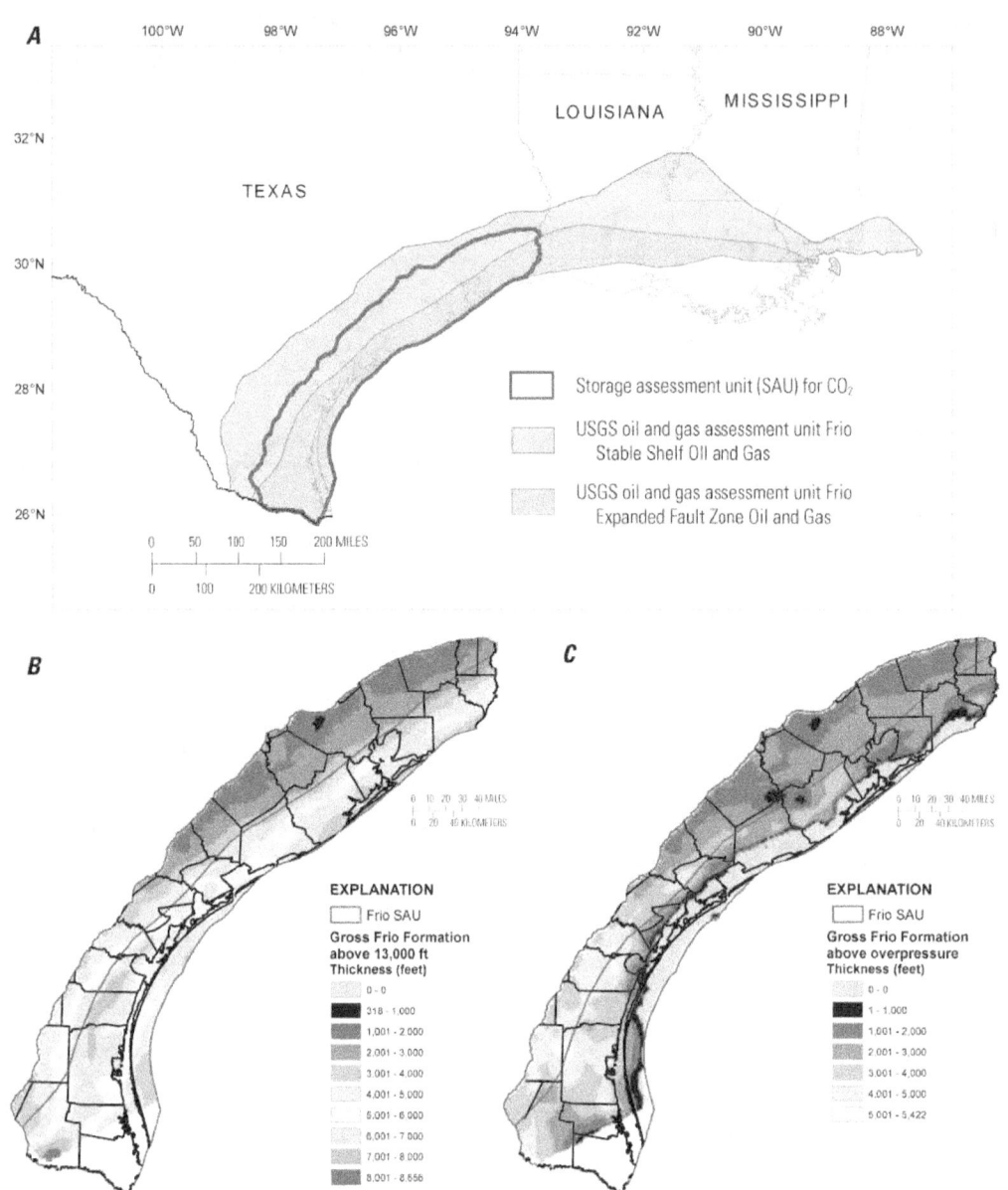

Figure 6.　Example of a storage assessment unit (SAU) for CO₂. *A,* SAU for the Frio Formation encompasses parts of two units defined for the USGS National Oil and Gas Assessment (NOGA): the Frio Stable Shelf Oil and Gas Assessment Unit and the Frio Expanded Fault Zone Oil and Gas Assessment Unit (U.S. Geological Survey, 2009). The SAU is constrained to the parts of the formation where the structure top (Swanson and Karlsen, 2009) is at least 3,000 ft below surface but above the lower depth limit of 13,000 ft. The Frio Formation test case is limited to Texas onshore and State waters. *B,* The gross formation thickness grid (Swanson and Karlsen, 2009) for the Frio Formation SAU excludes volumes at depths below 13,000 ft below the surface. *C,* The gross formation thickness grid for the Frio Formation SAU is revised also to exclude the overpressured zone derived from Wallace and others (1981). The presence of an overpressured zone can reduce the thickness to zero where the overpressure occurs above the top of the storage formation. In this example, the depth to the top of the overpressured zone is defined by the first occurrence of a pressure gradient of 0.5 pound per square inch per foot (lb/in²/ft).

2.1.3. Examples of Potential Additional Constraints

2.1.3.1. Subsurface Pressure

The lower depth limit of an SAU may be affected by the subsurface pressure regime. In relatively young sedimentary basins, such as the Gulf of Mexico, the pressures in formation fluids may exceed the hydrostatic pressure gradient (pressures commonly called overpressures), in some cases approaching the pressures due to lithostatic load (the black line labeled "Lithostatic gradient" in figure 5). Storage of CO_2 at overpressure conditions will be difficult due to additional compression needed to inject CO_2 at these conditions. Another limit to the technically accessible resource may be regulatory limits to injection pressure. For example, proposed regulations on CO_2 injection wells (U.S. Environmental Protection Agency, 2008) state that the injection pressure should not exceed 90 percent of the fracture pressure gradient for the lithology of the storage formation. The presence of naturally occurring overpressures may require injection pressures that are higher than this limit.

2.1.3.2. Formation Water Salinity

The U.S. standard for the salinity of drinking water is 500 milligrams per liter (mg/L) total dissolved solids (TDS), but any formation water with salinities lower than 10,000 mg/L TDS, regardless of depth, has the potential to be remediated and used as a potable water supply (U.S. Environmental Protection Agency, 2009). The U.S. Environmental Protection Agency (2008) has proposed the 10,000 mg/L TDS limit for injection of CO_2. Therefore, the potential storage resources for CO_2 in formations with salinities less than 10,000 mg/L TDS are not assessed in this methodology. Although salinities of formation water commonly increase with depth, it is possible that formation water within an assessment unit may be less saline than the 10,000 mg/L limit near the updip extent of the formation, eliminating a portion of the SAU.

2.1.4. Minimum Size

The concept of minimum size of technically accessible storage resources is important for probabilistic models of geologic resource assessment. A minimum accumulation size is used in the NOGA methodology as a way to eliminate any resource that will not be significant over the time span considered for the assessment. The minimum storage size used for this assessment methodology is 2 million cubic meters (approximately equivalent to 12.5 million petroleum barrels) of pore volume, which is equivalent to approximately 1 to 1.4 million metric tons of CO_2. This value represents the smallest potential storage size for an individual CO_2 storage project. However, a more relevant minimum storage size that could be used is

20 million metric tons of CO_2, as that represents the mass of CO_2 emissions from an individual industrial source generating 1 million metric tons of CO_2 per year over a timeframe of 20 years. An even larger minimum size could be 400 million metric tons of CO_2, the storage volume that is needed to store the cumulative emissions of a 1,000-megawatt coal-fired powerplant that is estimated to emit about 8 million metric tons of CO_2 per year (Brennan and Burruss, 2006) over the 50-year typical lifetime of a powerplant. By using probabilistic methods to evaluate the sizes and numbers of traps within an SAU, we can evaluate both the aggregate storage resource of the SAU and the probability that any trap or a fraction of the SF may retain at least a minimum storage mass required for deployment of carbon capture and storage (CCS) projects.

2.2. Trapping Processes

A number of processes will trap CO_2 in the subsurface. These include (1) physical trapping, or structural and stratigraphic trapping, of the buoyant phase below a seal or within a structure that has vertical and lateral permeability barriers (an oil and gas reservoir); (2) trapping by capillary forces in the pores of reservoir rocks on the trailing edge of the mobile CO_2 plume, typically referred to as capillary trapping and less commonly referred to as residual trapping; (3) solution trapping, where the CO_2 is dissolved in formation water, forming aqueous species such as H_2CO_3, HCO_3^-, and CO_3^{2-}; (4) dissolution trapping by dissolution in residual oil, mixing with residual gas, or solid organic matter (coal or kerogen) sorption; and (5) mineral trapping by precipitation of carbonate-bearing mineral phases, such as calcite, magnesite, siderite, and dawsonite. For development of this assessment methodology we focused on physical and capillary trapping and dissolution and mixing of CO_2 in formation water and residual hydrocarbons.

2.3. Seals

Seals (confining units, aquitards, cap rock) are regional geologic strata that inhibit the migration of fluids from adjacent geologic strata. The presence and adequacy of a seal is critical for defining a potential SAU for CO_2 sequestration. A seal may consist of single or multiple formations that have physical properties, usually defined by the lithofacies and burial history, that allow the retention of underlying fluids and gases. The petroleum industry has conducted extensive research on regional seal properties, seal behavior of faults, and the causes of seal failure (Skerlec, 1999; Couples, 2005; Hermanrud and others, 2005; Lowry, 2005; Nordgård Bolås and others, 2005). Assessment methods for geologic storage of CO_2 will require evaluation and prediction of seal integrity. Subsurface data from wells, formation tests, and laboratory measurements of rock properties are available from geographic regions with an extensive history of oil and gas exploration and production. Geologic provinces with sparse or poorly distributed measurements of seal properties may require additional measurements to assess seal integrity. Oil- and gas-producing basins are the most promising geologic provinces for CO_2 sequestration because geologists have data for the basins about lithology and depositional environment; extent, thickness, and integrity of top and fault seals; and the history of fluid migration.

2.3.1. Rock Types and Properties

Many rock types exhibit properties that can behave as a seal for CO_2 sequestration within the SAU as long as the seal unit or units have a wide geographic extent. Typical rock types that are documented as top seals include unfractured evaporites (halite, gypsum-anhydrite), mudrock (shale, mudstone, siltstone, claystone), argillaceous carbonate mudstone (clay-rich micrite), chert and other siliceous mudrock lithofacies, and some volcanic deposits such as basalt. Rock strata exhibiting the following physical properties can be effective seals: (1) sufficient geographic extent throughout a basin; (2) sufficient thickness, low permeability, and high capillary entry pressure to inhibit diffuse porous flow; and (3) sufficient ductility to deform plastically under strain without fracturing.

Mudrock, the most common seal for oil and gas traps, exhibits most or all of the necessary attributes to act as a regional seal. Within some sedimentary basins, thick, regionally extensive, fine-grained and very fine grained sandstone and siltstone with low permeability can serve as adequate seals under normal (hydrostatic) pressure gradients. Fine-grained carbonate, basalt, and chert are commonly brittle, rendering them susceptible to faulting and fracturing, resulting in high potential for seal failure. Evaporites, such as gypsum and anhydrite, exhibit ideal seal properties, but, in some areas, their geographic extent and thickness are limited. Where extensive salt deposits exist, such as deep below the U.S. Gulf Coast, salt could behave as an adequate seal; however, the depth and pressures may be prohibitive for CO_2 injection. Regional shale (or mudrock) layers associated with major marine transgressions (marine flooding surface) are very effective top seals in many passive margin continental settings with hydrocarbon accumulations.

2.3.2. Seal Integrity

Oil and gas exploration companies routinely study top seals and fault seal traps to predict which traps will hold hydrocarbon accumulations and which traps will not. Similar approaches need to be undertaken to understand seal integrity for the injection and storage of CO_2. The two primary pathways of fluids through a seal that may account for seal failure are (1) diffuse porous flow where the capillary entry-pressure of the seal is exceeded by the pore pressure as determined by the column height of the fluids (Hermanrud and others, 2005) and (2) leakage through fractures and faults. Diffuse porous flow is not considered to be a significant factor in the movement of fluids through seals (Couples, 2005). Flow simulations through mudrock seals suggest that CO_2 under Darcy flow is slow enough that the pore network of the seal retards vertical flow. However, sensitivity analysis of simulated fracture flow indicates that fractures are likely to serve as conduits for CO_2 migration (Cavanagh and others, 2006). Studies of seal fractures in oil and gas fields indicate that fracture flow accounts for large volumes of fluid movement through the seal. Skerlec (1999) estimated that a fracture with a permeability of 0.05 millidarcy (mD) in a seal overlying a typical North Sea field can leak more than 100 billion barrels per million years (or approximately 273 barrels per day).

Overpressured reservoirs can exceed the fracture pressure of the overlying seal, resulting in active fracturing and fluid flow during injection. Active fracturing is a potential hazard for CO_2 injection and may occur in a seal where the pore pressure in the trap, resulting from either the CO_2 injection rate or the height of the buoyant column of CO_2, exceeds the fracture pressure of the seal. For this reason, an understanding of the fracture pressure and burial history within a basin is important for evaluating a seal in an SAU.

Previously existing faults and fractures have the potential to be permeability barriers that act as seals or to be transmissive, allowing fluid flow across the fault or up the fault plane. Vertical migration along a fault plane or through an extensive fracture system within a seal formation may result in seal failure. Fault seals have been extensively investigated to understand hydrocarbon migration and trapping (Skerlec, 1999; Brown, 2003; Jones and Hillis, 2003; Couples, 2005; Hermanrud and others, 2005). Capillary entry pressures of faults are a significant parameter to determine the effectiveness of the fault seal. The integrity of the fault seal may be affected by the juxtaposition of the strata within the fault plane, fluid pressures, mineralogy, and geometry of the fault system. Fluid movement along faults can be inhibited by clay smear or shale gouge, cataclasis, or cementation of authigenic minerals such as quartz and dolomite (Gluyas and Swarbrick, 2004). Threshold ratios of shale to sand within the fault blocks and fault plane have been developed for specific basins to estimate the effectiveness of fault seals (Skerlec, 1999). For CO_2 sequestration, an approach analogous to oil and gas exploration will be needed to assess the effects of faults on fault seal integrity, sustainment of column height, and the potential for seal failure.

2.4. Subsurface Fluid Flow: Injection Rates, Displacement, and Other Flow Considerations Related to CO_2 Sequestration

Target formations for sequestration must accommodate CO_2 injection rates that are large enough to make full-scale sequestration practical without inducing large pressure changes that can fracture the rock. Characterizing the ability to maintain large CO_2 injection rates requires consideration of time-varying fluid flow in porous media and accompanying changes in fluid storage. Injected fluid is accommodated by (1) fluid compression, (2) expansion of the pores, and (3) displacement of fluids already in the pores. These processes may occur simultaneously in the same volume of rock as a result of fluid pressure increases.

Confining layers (seals and low-permeability interbedded strata) adjoining aquifers can accept large volumes of fluid displaced during injection. As a result, pressure increases during injection (fig. 7) are strongly controlled by confining layer properties. In formations from which water, oil, or gas have been extracted, system behavior during extraction may provide information about the confining layers. In many situations, however, little is known about confining layer hydraulic behavior and even the large-scale connectedness and behavior of the aquifer are unknown. Research to improve characterization of these flow-controlling aspects of subsurface systems is crucial to incorporate flow aspects into future updates of this methodology and any large-scale CO_2 injection efforts.

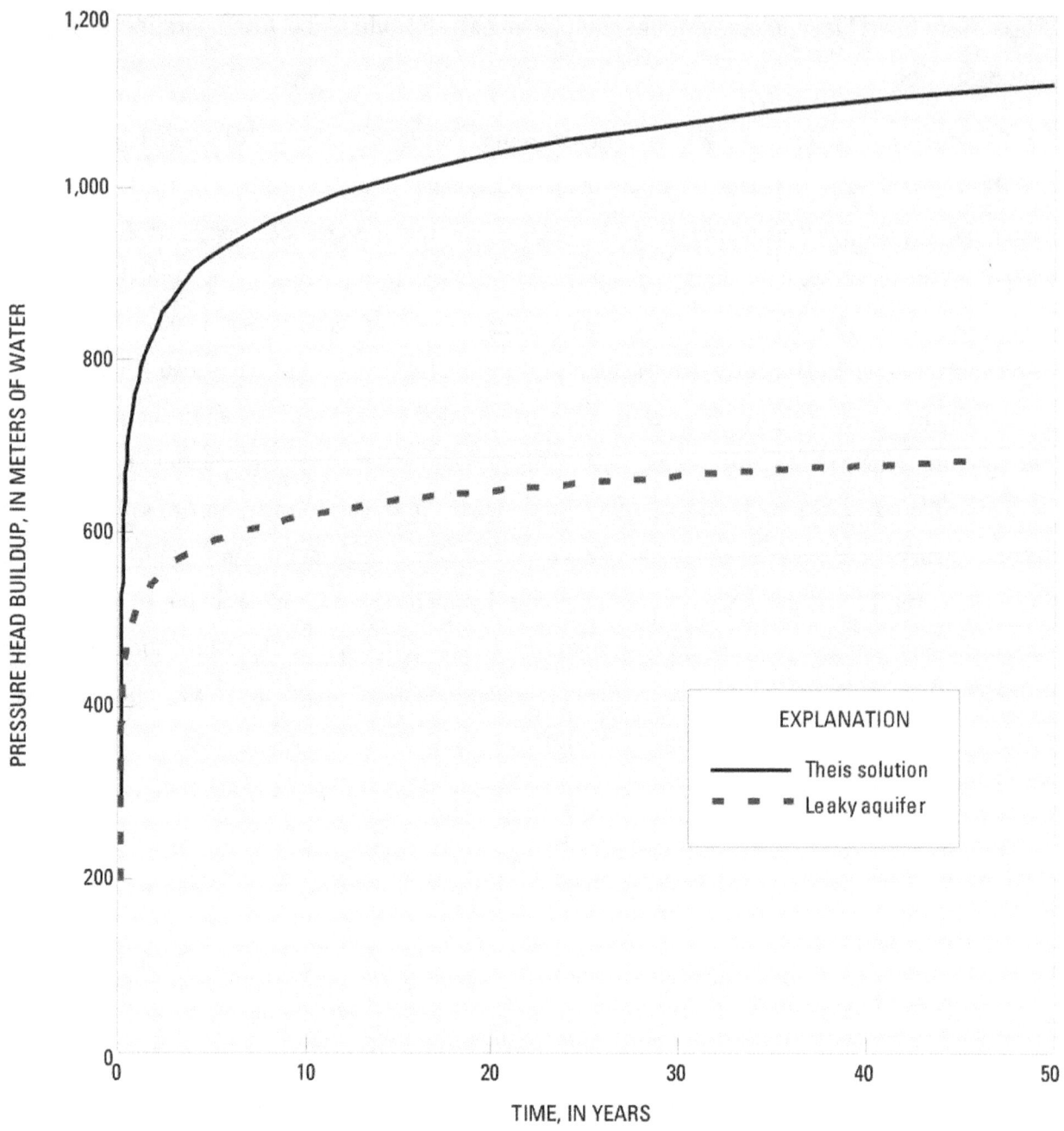

Figure 7. Simulated pressure head buildup versus time in an injection well in a hypothetical aquifer. The Theis (1935) solution is calculated according to an assumption that the aquifer confining layers are impermeable, whereas the so-called "leaky aquifer" solution allows movement of water into the confining layers. The curves are based on the following assumed values: an injection rate of 1.5×10^7 m³ per year; an aquifer hydraulic conductivity and specific storage of 7.4×10^{-6} m/s and 1.0×10^{-6} 1/m, respectively; and, for the "leaky aquifer" case, a confining layer hydraulic diffusivity of 3.0×10^{-6} m²/s. Abbreviations are as follows: m² = square meters, m³ = cubic meters. m²/s = square meters per second, 1/m = inverse meters.

2.5. Geochemical Processes Associated with CO_2 Sequestration in Geologic Formations

2.5.1. CO_2 Reactions with Reservoir and Seal over Time

Injected CO_2 may react with reservoir and seal rocks, causing dissolution, precipitation, and transformation of minerals that may result in changes in porosity and permeability (Hepple and Benson, 2005; Xu and others, 2005; Kharaka and others, 2006) and potentially affecting the probability of containment of CO_2. Geochemical reactions with formation water and reservoir and seal rocks begin immediately upon injection of supercritical CO_2 and continue until the system reaches equilibrium, probably on the time scale of tens of thousands of years [fig. 8 (Benson and Cook, 2005)].

During injection (Han, 2008; Han and McPherson, 2008), the bulk of the CO_2 will be stored as a supercritical fluid by structural and stratigraphic trapping. Some of the CO_2 will dissolve in formation water, causing solution trapping through the formation of aqueous species such as H_2CO_3, HCO_3^-, and CO_3^{2-}. Initially, the total content of dissolved CO_2 species in formation brines will be in the range of 1 to 5 percent by brine weight (Spycher and Pruess, 2005). According to computer modeling, capillary trapping of CO_2 in the pores of reservoir rocks trailing the supercritical plume is likely to be volumetrically limited during the injection phase of a sequestration project (Han and McPherson, 2008).

Through time, residual, solution, and mineral trapping will become the dominant storage phases (figs. 8 and 9), thereby increasing storage containment. The amount of CO_2 sequestered in each phase will be dependent on reactivity of the reservoir minerals, the chemical composition of the formation water, and reservoir pressure and temperature (Hitchon, 1996; Knauss and others, 2005; Perry and others, 2007; Han and McPherson, 2008).

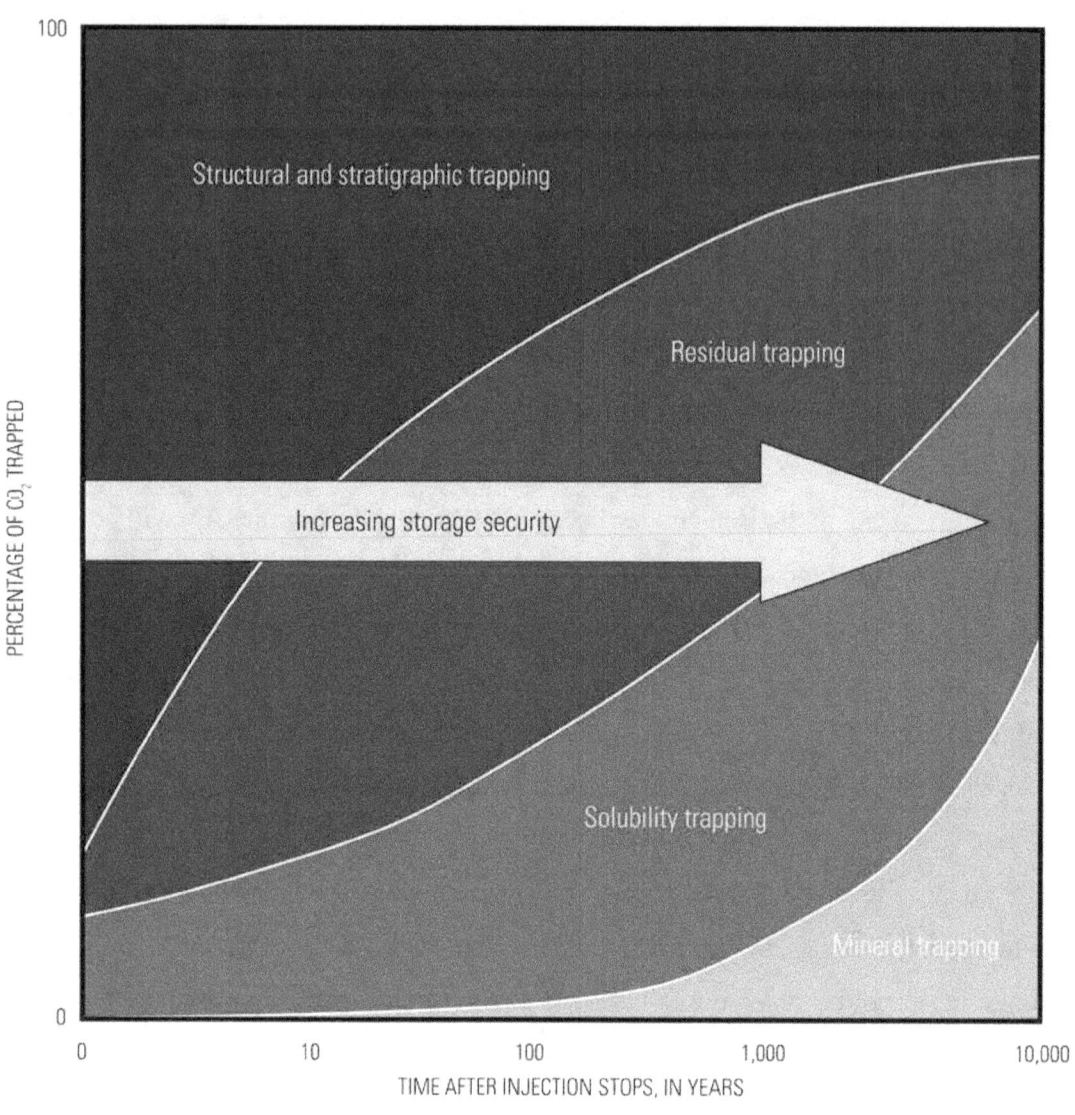

Figure 8. Schematic diagram illustrating CO_2 storage types through 10,000 years (from Benson and Cook, 2005). The term solubility trapping here is synonymous with the term solution trapping used in the text.

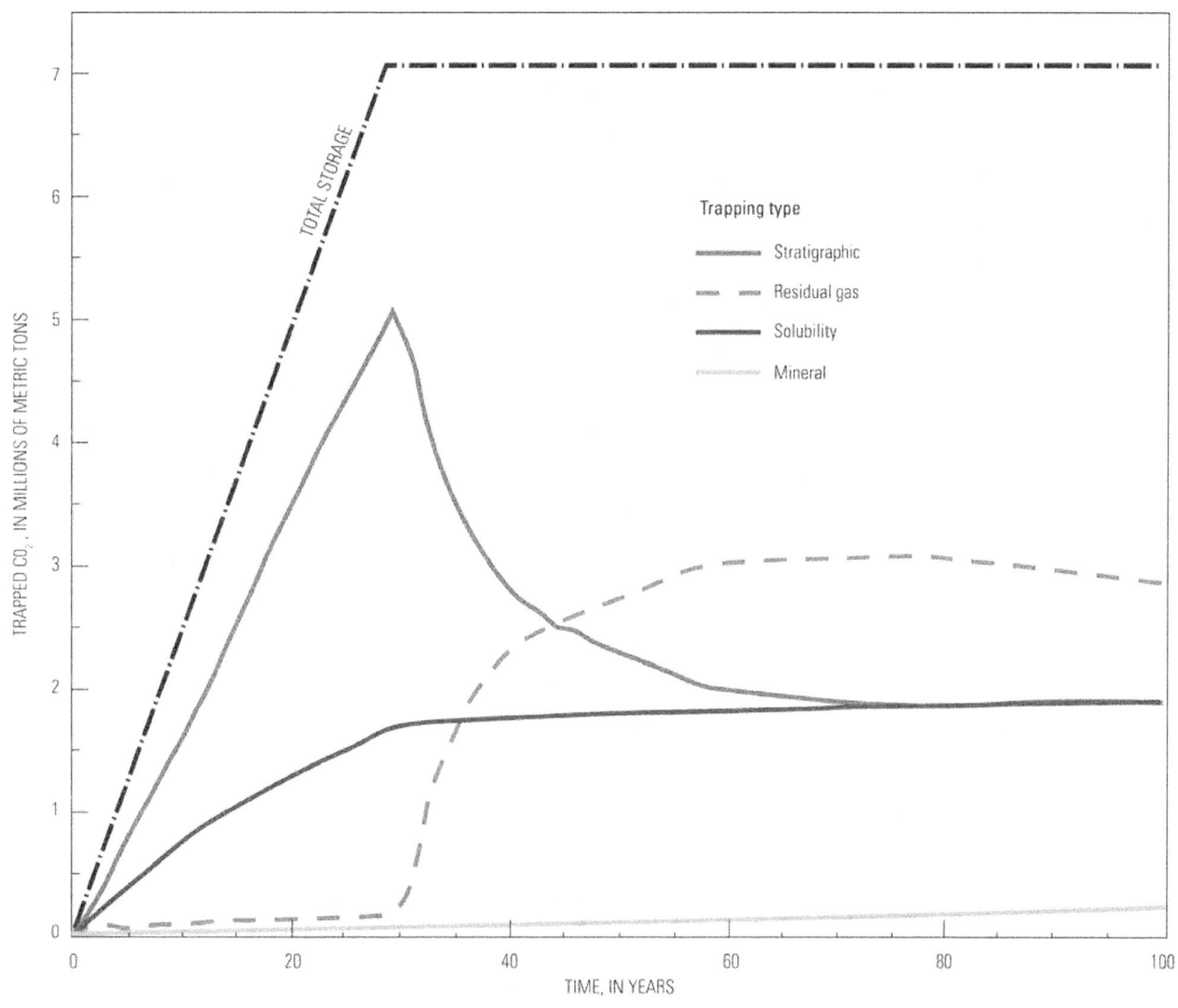

Figure 9. Relative types of trapping for injected CO_2, over 100 years, from a numerical model of the SACROC unit of the Kelly-Snyder field, western Texas. During the first 30 years of the simulation, CO_2 is injected for enhanced oil recovery (EOR). The remaining time in the modeled results shows the response of the system with no additional injection. Modified from Han (2008).

2.5.2. Geochemical Reactions

Experimental measurements and equations of state for CO_2 and brines indicate that CO_2 solubility increases with decreasing salinity of formation water, increasing the ratio of dissolved calcium (Ca) to sodium (Na) and increasing pressure of CO_2. CO_2 solubility decreases with increasing temperature to about 150°C and then increases at higher temperatures (Duan and Sun, 2003; Rosenbauer and others, 2005). Computer simulations, laboratory experiments, and field tests indicate that the amount of CO_2 sequestered by mineral trapping (Gunter and others, 1997; Hellevang and others, 2005; Palandri and others, 2005; Perry and others, 2007) is primarily dependent on the reactivity of the reservoir minerals but affected by the chemical composition of the formation water and reservoir temperature and pressure (Hitchon, 1996; Knauss and others, 2005; Perry and others, 2007; Han and McPherson, 2008). Injection of CO_2 into limestone reservoirs will result in relatively rapid dissolution of carbonate minerals to saturation with calcite and a ~2-percent increase in porosity (Emberley and others, 2005; Rosenbauer and others, 2005). Kharaka and others (2006, 2009) showed that injection of CO_2 into arkosic sandstone initially lowered pH values (as low as ~3.0) leading to dissolution of calcite and iron oxyhydroxides. Their geochemical simulations indicated that brine pH would increase over time as a result of the slower dissolution of feldspar minerals (oligoclase), leading to the precipitation of calcite, dawsonite, and other minerals over time (Kharaka and others, 2006, 2009). More carbonate minerals would ultimately precipitate from sandstones with more feldspar minerals and where the feldspars were more calcic (for example, anorthite). Reactive siliceous reservoir and seal rocks that contain high concentrations of magnesium, iron, and calcium (Mg, Fe, and Ca) can sequester high volumes of CO_2 as carbonate minerals.

Abundant relevant and detailed information exists on the chemical composition of formation water produced with oil and gas and obtained from drill-stem tests and other fluid sampling procedures carried out on exploration wells (see Kharaka and Hanor, 2007, for a recent review and list of references). The USGS produced-waters database (Breit, 2002) contains chemical data for approximately 70,000 U.S. wells, which can be used to determine salinities and chemical composition of formation waters for CO_2 storage assessments in the United States.

2.6. Storage Efficiency

The storage efficiency factor is the fraction of the total pore volume of a PT or the SF that will be occupied by CO_2. In practice, this value is not well known and is given as a distribution that reflects the range and most likely value of the parameter. The distribution of values may have significantly different ranges depending on the dominant trapping processes and whether storage occurs in the PTs or the SF of an SAU. The storage efficiency is the sum of the fractions of storage due to each trapping mechanism (buoyancy, capillarity, dissolution, solubility, mineralization). For example, in a PT within a storage formation with homogeneous porosity and permeability, trapping will be dominated by buoyancy. The maximum fraction of the porosity in the trap that can be filled with CO_2 is the complement of the irreducible water saturation due to gravity drainage. In this case, storage efficiency will have relatively high values and may range from 0.4 to 0.8. However, if the storage formation in the PT has a heterogeneous distribution of flow properties with large variations in permeability on relatively short length scales, then storage may be dominated by capillarity and solubility. This situation will decrease storage efficiency to a range on the order of 0.05 to 0.20. In the SFs, physical trapping due to buoyancy may be of limited importance, with trapping dominated by capillarity, solubility, and mineralization. Each of these trapping processes retains a relatively small amount of CO_2 per unit of storage formation, resulting in storage efficiencies on the order of 0.01 to 0.05 (U.S. Department of Energy, National Energy Technology Laboratory, 2008a). However, the uncertainty in storage efficiency in SFs may be larger than this range because the processes that retain CO_2 within SFs are not as well understood as the processes in PTs.

In traps where buoyancy is the dominant trapping mechanism, the fraction of pore space that will be occupied by CO_2 can be reduced by any factor that causes the buoyant fluid to escape from the PT, such as failure of the seal or the presence of transmissive faults. Capillary trapping of CO_2 will occur only in portions of the rock that the CO_2 plume has moved through. The movement of a CO_2 plume is by nature anisotropic, because the storage formation is heterogeneous. Therefore, the CO_2 plume will interact with the portions of the storage formation that have relatively higher transmissivities than the rest of the storage formation. Furthermore, the fraction of pore space occupied by CO_2 via capillary trapping will be a function of the heterogeneity in the distribution of porosity within the storage formation (Doughty and others, 2007). Similarly, the fraction of pore space occupied by CO_2 via solution, dissolution, or mineral trapping will also be determined by heterogeneity, as all of these processes are dependent on the interaction of the CO_2 plume with formation fluids and minerals.

The maximum values for storage efficiency assume ideal trapping conditions for all storage types. Factors that control the minimum values for the storage efficiency distribution in PTs are any geologic or hydrologic process that reduces pore volume available for CO_2 storage. For storage determined by fluid production, the minimum efficiency values are controlled by factors such as recharge of formation water that refills pore space or compaction of the formation reducing pore volume. In addition, any process that reduces the size of the trap, such as seal failure, transmissive faults, or well bore failure, will reduce the storage efficiency of the PTs.

The storage processes in SFs are different than those in PTs in that the relative percentage of CO_2 trapped as a buoyant fluid may be much lower in SFs. Other processes such as capillary, solution, and dissolution trapping in SFs may be more important than in PTs. The uncertainty in storage efficiency in SFs may be large because the processes that retain CO_2 within SFs are not as well understood as processes in PTs. Similar to the previous discussion of the impact of heterogeneity on plume migration, capillary trapping, and other trapping processes, the heterogeneity of the SF may be a critical factor in estimating the storage efficiency of SFs. However, all the factors that control storage efficiency in PTs, such as the seal, faults, and well failure, must also be factored into the storage efficiency estimate for SFs.

3. Storage Resource Classification and Estimation

The probabilistic methods used in this assessment methodology are based on the methods developed over many years by USGS geoscientists for assessment of undiscovered, technically recoverable oil and gas resources (referred to here as "NOGA methods", where NOGA stands for the USGS National Oil and Gas Assessment). Two types of NOGA methods are relevant to CO_2 storage assessment: (1) conventional petroleum accumulation assessments and (2) deposit simulation assessments. Both methods estimate resource in conventional accumulations at the assessment unit (AU) or play level, where the goal is estimation of the aggregate volume of resource within an estimated number and size distribution of discrete, undiscovered, conventional accumulations (Schmoker and Klett, 2000). The NOGA conventional petroleum accumulation assessment method is used in basins that have a history of oil and gas exploration and development, with adequate statistics to apply discovery process modeling (Drew, 1990, 1997; Drew and Schuenemeyer, 1993; Houghton and others, 1993). The NOGA deposit simulation model is used in USGS evaluations of oil and gas resources in the North Slope of Alaska, where there are significant limitations on data available from historical exploration and development and the amount of geological information is also limited (Schuenemeyer, 2005). Both methods can take into account additional geologic factors that may limit the chance of successful discovery of resources greater than a minimum size – the overall evaluation of these factors is expressed as a probability of success (evaluation of risk). The resource estimated without taking into account these geologic factors is referred to as the conditional resource, whereas the resource estimated accounting for these geologic factors is referred to as the unconditional resource. The two methods differ on how the unconditional resource is determined. The NOGA conventional methodology unconditional resource takes into account the possibility that there might be no recoverable resource in the entire AU greater than some minimum size. In contrast, the deposit simulation methodology provides for the evaluation of success at two levels: (1) a probability that the entire play may not contain a deposit that meets the minimum size: and (2) a probability that individual deposits may not meet the minimum size.

The CO_2 storage resource assessment methodology adapts these NOGA methods to the evaluation of technically accessible storage resource. Both conditional and unconditional resources are evaluated as described below.

3.1. Storage Types for Volumetric Calculation Methods

3.1.1. Physical Trap Model and Storage Volumes

Discovered traps (PT_{DS}) within a SAU are the oil and gas reservoirs within the flow unit of the SAU that have a history of oil and gas production. In this storage type, retention of free-phase CO_2 by a seal is the dominant trapping mechanism, although dissolution trapping in the residual oil phase and residual formation water also occur. Because hydrocarbons were present and produced from the PT_D, an effective seal is present, and the production history provides information about the flow properties of the PT_D. If there is evidence of seal failure or problems with fluid flow in the PT_D, then this information can be incorporated into the factors used to evaluate containment success. The data gathered on the PT_{DS} can be used to make inferences about the properties of the PT_{US}. The numbers and sizes of undiscovered conventional accumulations estimated for NOGA AUs can be used in conjunction with the data from the PT_{DS} to create the data distributions required for the CO_2 storage resource input form.

Four types of storage resources can be estimated in PTs. Each type can be evaluated in this methodology. The formulas and inputs used to calculate the volumes of resource in each type of storage are given in table 1 and discussed in later sections of this report.

Table 1. Volumetric formulas for discovered physical traps (PT_{DS}).

[Symbols are defined in the table footnotes]

Calculation method	Storage type	Formula
A	Conventional EOR, S_{EOR}	$= OOIP * I_R * C_{EOR}$
B	Net cumulative volume, NCV, S_{NCV}	$= NCV * C_{WD} * C_{F1} * \rho_{CO2}$
C	Total known volume, S_{TKV}	$= T_A * T_I * N_{TP} * \phi * C_{SE} * C_{F2} * \rho_{CO2}$
D	Total trap volume, S_{TTV}	$= S_{TKV} * C_G$

OOIP: volume of original oil in place (OOIP) in petroleum barrels. If values are not available, OOIP can be calculated from the cumulative volume of produced hydrocarbon liquids by using a recovery factor. The equation for calculating OOIP follows: OOIP $= CV_{OC} / R_F$.

CV_{OC}: cumulative volume of produced hydrocarbon liquids in reservoirs that are classified as oil accumulations (oil (O) + condensate (C) in petroleum barrels).

R_F: oil recovery factor (fraction).

I_R: incremental recovery of OOIP induced by CO_2 enhanced-oil-recovery (EOR) methods (fraction).

C_{EOR}: storage efficiency of conventional EOR, in metric tons of CO_2 retained in the reservoir per barrel of incremental oil recovered (fraction).

NCV: net cumulative volume of reservoir fluid produced, in barrels at subsurface conditions. See text for discussion of conversion of volume of produced gas to subsurface volume in barrels.

C_{WD}: correction factor for potential refilling of trap by natural water recharge or water flooding during oil recovery (fraction). This may limit the fraction of the trap that can be filled with CO_2 (see discussion in Shaw and Bachu, 2002).

C_{F1}: conversion factor, petroleum barrels (42 gallons) to cubic meters (m^3): 0.159 bbl/m^3

ρ_{CO2}: density of CO_2 in metric tons per cubic meter (metric tons/m^3).

T_A: trap area from which hydrocarbons and water have been produced, in acres, defined by production well locations.

T_I: interval thickness of storage formation, in feet.

N_{TP}: fraction of T_I, with porosity greater than the minimum used for evaluation of petroleum resources (fraction). The product (T_I* N_{TP}) is commonly called "net pay," "net productive interval," or "net porous interval."

Φ: porosity (fraction).

C_{SE}: storage efficiency factor; that fraction of the pore space that can be occupied by CO_2. In PTs, this value should approach the complement of the irreducible water saturation.

C_{F2}: conversion factor, acre-feet to cubic meters (m^3) = 1,233.5 m^3/acre-ft.

C_G: growth factor, accounting for the potential that the area of the trap that produced hydrocarbons, TA, may be less than the area of the trap to the spill point. Default value is 1.0 (no growth), but if values can be estimated from geologic information, they should be >1.0.

PTs that are classified as oil reservoirs have the gas:oil ratio (GOR) less than 20,000 cubic feet per barrel (cf/bbl); for such PTs, one type of storage resource is related to the net CO_2 left in place following conventional CO_2 EOR practice (water-alternating-gas injection) (J.P. Meyer, Contek Solutions, Plano, Tex., written commun., 2009). This is called conventional EOR storage (S_{EOR}). This estimate of storage is typically the smallest storage resource assigned to a specific trap. However, CO_2 injection for EOR is a proven technology that is currently in use in oil fields. Furthermore, EOR can be initiated in oil fields prior to depletion without damaging the resource, providing a CO_2 storage technology that could be deployed today.

Another type of storage resource in PTs is based on the net cumulative volume (NCV) of oil, gas, and water produced from the PT_D. This is S_{NCV}. The NCV is the cumulative volume of fluid production (oil, gas, and water) minus the volume of fluid injected (water and gas) over the production history of the PT_D. Accurate calculation of NCV (commonly called fluid balance in the petroleum engineering literature) requires correction of the volumes of the fluids measured at surface conditions to the volumes that they occupied in the subsurface through the use of formation volume factors for each fluid. If there has been no natural water recharge (water drive) or water injection into the PT_D, and no evidence of loss of porosity due to compaction after fluid extraction, then the NCV may be the storage resource with the least uncertainty. If there is some evidence of natural water drive or the reservoir has undergone secondary recovery by waterflooding, then this volume must be modified by a correction factor, C_{WD}, that accounts for the fraction of pore space that is "refilled" by water that cannot be displaced by injected CO_2 (Shaw and Bachu, 2002). This storage resource is not applicable to PT_{US}, which are, by definition, undiscovered and have not had any fluid removed or injected. Therefore, PT_{US} are not considered for the NCV calculation.

A third type of storage resource, the total known volume (TKV), is based on the total volume of pore space within the area of an oil and gas reservoir, called S_{TKV}. The volume is calculated by using the area of the reservoir as defined by the locations of the wells that produced fluids from that reservoir, the net sand reservoir thickness beneath the field, the porosity, and a correction factor, C_{SE}, where "SE" stands for storage efficiency, that accounts for the fraction of pore space that can be occupied by injected CO_2. Once all recoverable hydrocarbons have been removed from the trap, especially in pressure-depleted gas fields, the upper limit on C_{SE} is related to the irreducible water saturation of the trap in the presence of CO_2. Values for irreducible water saturation in petroleum reservoirs are not well known, but they probably range from a minimum of about 0.2 in gas reservoirs to about 0.6 in oil reservoirs (Craft and Hawkins, 1991). Therefore, reasonable values for C_{SE} in TKV should range from 0.8 to 0.4 for CO_2 storage in PTs. If it is possible to establish a correlation between the area of a reservoir and the volume of technically recoverable hydrocarbons, then the number and sizes of undiscovered fields estimated in NOGA for the AU can be used to estimate the storage resource of the PT_{US}.

A fourth type of storage is called the total trap volume (TTV). This is the storage resource of the PT if we had complete knowledge of the structure of the trap so that the volume of the trap to the spill point can be defined. If all traps in a SAU were filled to the spill point, then TTV should equal TKV. However, we know that many petroleum traps are not completely filled, so that TKV is some fraction of TTV. If there is geologic evidence of the extent of trap fill within an SAU, then a trap fill factor can be defined and applied to the TKV to determine TTV. In the absence of any data on the extent of trap fill, then it may be appropriate to ignore this type of storage volume. By doing so, some part of this "missing fraction" of trap volume automatically is assigned to the volume of the SF.

3.1.2. Saline Formation Model and Storage Volumes

The saline formation (SF) is the CO_2 storage portion of the flow unit of the SAU that has no PTs greater than the minimum size. The CO_2 will be trapped in the SF primarily by capillary forces; however, buoyant trapping is also likely due to filling of small undiscovered traps and heterogeneity in fluid flow caused by natural permeability differences within geologic strata.

The SF within the SAU is the remainder of the flow unit not assessed by the PT methodology. For this methodology, the SF is defined by the areal extent of the SAU, minus the PT_D area, and an estimate of the distribution of the PT_U area. Known regions of the SAU that are not suitable for SF storage must be removed, for example, known areas of salt or shale diapirs, igneous intrusions, or other nonflow-unit intrusions. If there are no oil or gas production data, or no NOGA estimates of PT_{US}, then the entire SAU is considered an SF.

For the purposes of this methodology, it is assumed that CO_2 will be stored only within the most porous interval of a storage formation. Porous interval thickness is commonly referred to as the "net sand" or "pay zone" or "porous interval"; for this methodology, it is referred to as the "net porous interval." The net porous interval thickness is used to define the volume of storage within the SF. Therefore, some estimate of the thickness of this porous rock is needed. Because of the natural variations in ranges of porosity between potential SAUs throughout the United States and the world, the minimum porosity used to estimate the thickness of the net porous interval must be defined by the assessment geologist using available data for the formations in the SAU.

The storage resource calculation for the SF is similar to volumetric resource, or TKV, of the PTs, in that it is based on the total volume of pore space in the entire SF. The volume of resource is calculated from the area, thickness, porosity, and storage efficiency. The assessment geologist calculates the mean values for the area, thickness, and porosity for the entire SF and then estimates the uncertainty of each of those mean values. The goal is to determine how representative the mean values are for the entire SF. As the area of the SF is typically clearly defined, the uncertainty in the mean area of the SF is small. The mean values for thickness and porosity of the SF are calculated by using the values gathered from the research for the framework geology of the SAU. However, the thickness and porosity data may be primarily from the PTs, in which case there could be significant uncertainty about whether the mean values calculated from those data accurately represent the SFs. The storage efficiency should be determined by the assessment geologist on the basis of the quality of the first three inputs; however, this distribution is difficult to quantify. In the case studies used to develop this methodology, a range of storage efficiency factors from a minimum of 0.01 to a maximum of 0.05 is used. This range is based on previously published estimates (van der Meer, 1995; U.S. Department of Energy, National Energy Technology Laboratory, 2008a).

3.2. Probabilistic Calculations

3.2.1. Probabilistic Calculations for Discovered Physical Traps

Formulas for estimating the four types of storage resource in PTs are given in table 1. These formulas convert trap volume to storage resource in metric tons of CO_2. For any set of PTs, the storage resource can be calculated deterministically and the individual masses summed to give an aggregate storage resource of PT_{DS} within an SAU. However, many of the parameters have significant uncertainties or ranges of measured values that should be incorporated into the calculations to clearly show the limits of our knowledge of potential storage resources. Over time, as our knowledge of volumetric factors in individual SAUs improves, the uncertainties should decrease, and the range of possible values of storage resources will narrow and more accurately represent the storage resource. The ranges of values and uncertainties can be incorporated into the volumetric calculations with Monte Carlo simulation techniques (Charpentier and Klett, 2005). The result is a probability distribution of all possible storage sizes of individual PT_{DS} for a given set of input parameters for a specific type of storage. This size distribution can then be used with a distribution of the number of PT_{DS} that are being considered for storage. This number distribution is limited by a minimum storage size parameter and may be, for example, a single number, such as 50 PT_{DS} with greater than 20 million metric tons of storage or, for an SAU with a limited number of PT_{DS}, simply the total number of PT_{DS}.

These two distributions, the sizes of possible storage and the number of PT_{DS}, are equivalent to the two inputs used in the USGS Monte Carlo simulator for calculating undiscovered, conventional oil and gas resources. These inputs are the size and number distribution of undiscovered accumulations of oil or gas. The output of the simulator is a probability distribution of the aggregate volume of the undiscovered resource and a distribution of sizes of the largest possible undiscovered accumulation. In the present case of estimation of storage resources, the inputs are known distributions, but the calculation is exactly the same, in this case with the output being a distribution of the possible sizes of the aggregate storage resource and a distribution of the sizes of the largest possible storage resource in a single PT_D. The sequence of calculations is shown in figure 10.

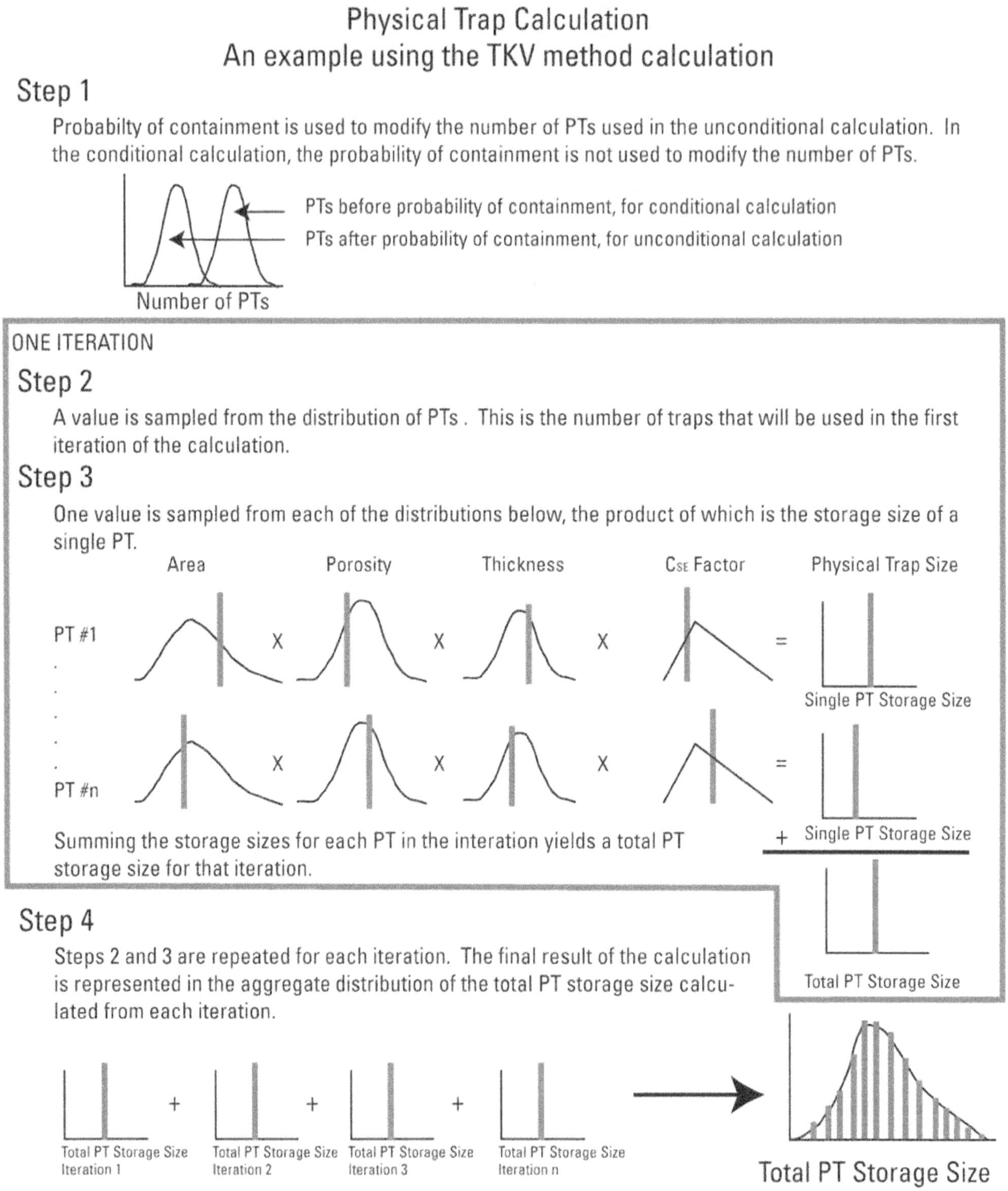

Physical Trap Calculation
An example using the TKV method calculation

Step 1

Probabilty of containment is used to modify the number of PTs used in the unconditional calculation. In the conditional calculation, the probability of containment is not used to modify the number of PTs.

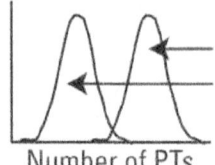

PTs before probability of containment, for conditional calculation

PTs after probability of containment, for unconditional calculation

Number of PTs

ONE ITERATION

Step 2

A value is sampled from the distribution of PTs . This is the number of traps that will be used in the first iteration of the calculation.

Step 3

One value is sampled from each of the distributions below, the product of which is the storage size of a single PT.

| Area | Porosity | Thickness | C$_{SE}$ Factor | Physical Trap Size |

PT #1   X   X   X   =

Single PT Storage Size

PT #n   X   X   X   =

+ Single PT Storage Size

Summing the storage sizes for each PT in the interation yields a total PT storage size for that iteration.

Total PT Storage Size

Step 4

Steps 2 and 3 are repeated for each iteration. The final result of the calculation is represented in the aggregate distribution of the total PT storage size calculated from each iteration.

Total PT Storage Size Iteration 1   +   Total PT Storage Size Iteration 2   +   Total PT Storage Size Iteration 3   +   Total PT Storage Size Iteration n

Total PT Storage Size

Figure 10. A flow diagram illustrating how the aggregate physical trap (PT) storage distribution is generated from the input values on the PT form (appendix A.1). TKV method, total known volume method, which is method C in table 1; C$_{SE}$, storage efficiency factor.

The basic concept of modeling the aggregate storage resource of PT_{DS} can be illustrated with geologically realistic cumulative production data for a hypothetical SAU that contains 400 PT_{DS} that meet the minimum size limit of 2 million m^3 of potential storage volume. Table 2 lists cumulative production data and approximate net cumulative volume in barrels for 10 PT_{DS} that are classified as oil or gas fields. Of the 400 hypothetical PT_{DS}, 50 have an estimated storage resource as NCV that is greater than 20 million metric tons CO_2, and 25 of those are classified as oil reservoirs (GOR less than 20,000 cf/bbl) for which a storage estimate from EOR is meaningful. Table 3 lists the input parameters used in the probabilistic calculation of the distribution of possible CO_2 storage in the 25 PT_{DS} due to conventional EOR. A probability distribution of the range of masses of CO_2 storage in the PT_{DS} is shown in figure 11. This range of sizes of possible storage is equivalent to the range of sizes of undiscovered oil and gas accumulations that is used in the NOGA methodology to estimate the technically recoverable resource of undiscovered oil and gas in a NOGA assessment unit.

Table 2. Realistic cumulative fluid production and injection data for 10 large discovered physical traps (PT_{DS}) in a hypothetical storage assessment unit (SAU) containing 400 PT_{DS} that exceed the minimum size of 12.5 million barrels (2 million cubic meters).

[ID, identifier; Cum., cumulative; MCF, thousand cubic feet; bbl, barrel; --, none.]

PT ID	PT area, acres	Cum. gas production, 10³ MCF	Cum. gas injection, 10³ MCF	Cum. water injection, 10³ bbl	Cum. water production, 10³ bbl	Cum. oil production, 10³ bbl	Cum. condensate production, 10³ bbl	Approximate net cumulative volume (NCV), 10³ bbl	Field type
3	31,400	4,798,900	--	10,000	26,300	99,100	32,000	4,946,300	Gas
4	50,100	1,978,500	0.003	969,000	2,237,300	808,700	415	4,055,915	Oil
14	14,500	500,300	478	617,700	811,100	284,000	419	977,641	Oil
15	16,700	809,600	617	5,400	36,600	114	1,000	841,297	Gas
22	24,200	225,000	--	12,500	246,500	101,500	3,000	563,500	Oil
23	15,600	484,500	--	5,100	27,400	18,800	1,400	527,000	Gas
24	8,900	513,600	--	800	5,000	415	1,700	519,915	Gas
30	14,300	275,400	--	79,100	159,200	64,000	1,300	420,800	Oil
48	2,600	19,400	--	60,100	269,200	33,300	11,800	273,600	Oil
49	8,700	262,600	2,500	4,700	1,800	--	0.083	257,200	Gas

Table 3. Input parameters for probabilistic calculation of S_{EOR} for 25 large discovered physical traps (PT$_{DS}$) that produced oil in a hypothetical, but geologically realistic, storage assessment unit (SAU).

[The production data for the 5 PT$_{DS}$ in table 2 that are classified as oil fields are part of the set of inputs included in the distributions in this table. Ranges of values for I_R and C_{EOR} were provided by J.P. Meyer, (Contek Solutions, Plano, Tex., written commun., 2009). Terms are discussed in section 3.1.1. C_{EOR}, storage based on CO_2 enhanced-oil-recovery (EOR) methods; CV_{OC}, cumulative volume of produced hydrocarbon liquids in oil accumulations]

Input parameters	Shape of the distribution of values	Most likely	Minimum	Maximum
Cumulative oil recovery, CV_{OC}, in barrels	Log-normal	110,000,000	3,000,000	980,000,000
Oil recovery factor, R_F	Triangular	0.44	0.16	0.68
EOR incremental recovery factor, I_R	Triangular	0.15	0.07	0.23
EOR CO_2 storage factor, C_{EOR}, in metric tons/barrel	Triangular	0.36	0.13	0.58

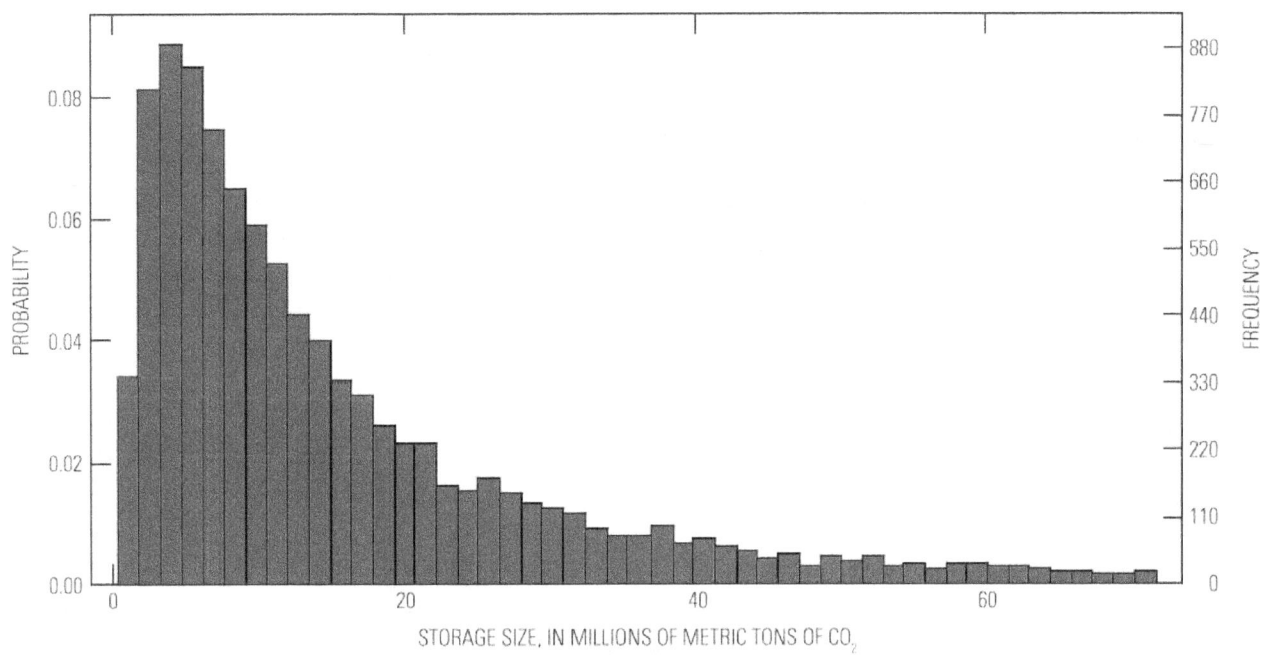

Figure 11. Probability distribution of storage size in any one of 25 large discovered physical traps (PT$_{DS}$) due to conventional EOR in a hypothetical storage assessment unit (SAU). The distribution is calculated with Crystal Ball™ for 10,000 iterations of the formula for method A in table 1 using the distributions of input parameters listed in table 3.

The hypothetical size distribution shown in figure 11 can be used with the number of PT_Ds (25) to make a probabilistic estimate of the CO_2 storage resource due to conventional EOR. We have not written a probabilistic algorithm specifically for CO_2 storage calculations. However, because we have a calculated size distribution and a number of PT_Ds, these values can be used with existing USGS probabilistic algorithms for calculating the volume of undiscovered oil and gas resources (Charpentier and Klett, 2005). An example of the probability distribution of the aggregate mass of CO_2 storage resource due to conventional EOR for a hypothetical SAU is shown in figure 12, and 95th, 50th, and 5th percentiles of occurrence of the technically accessible storage resource in 25 traps with a hypothetical SAU are given in table 4.

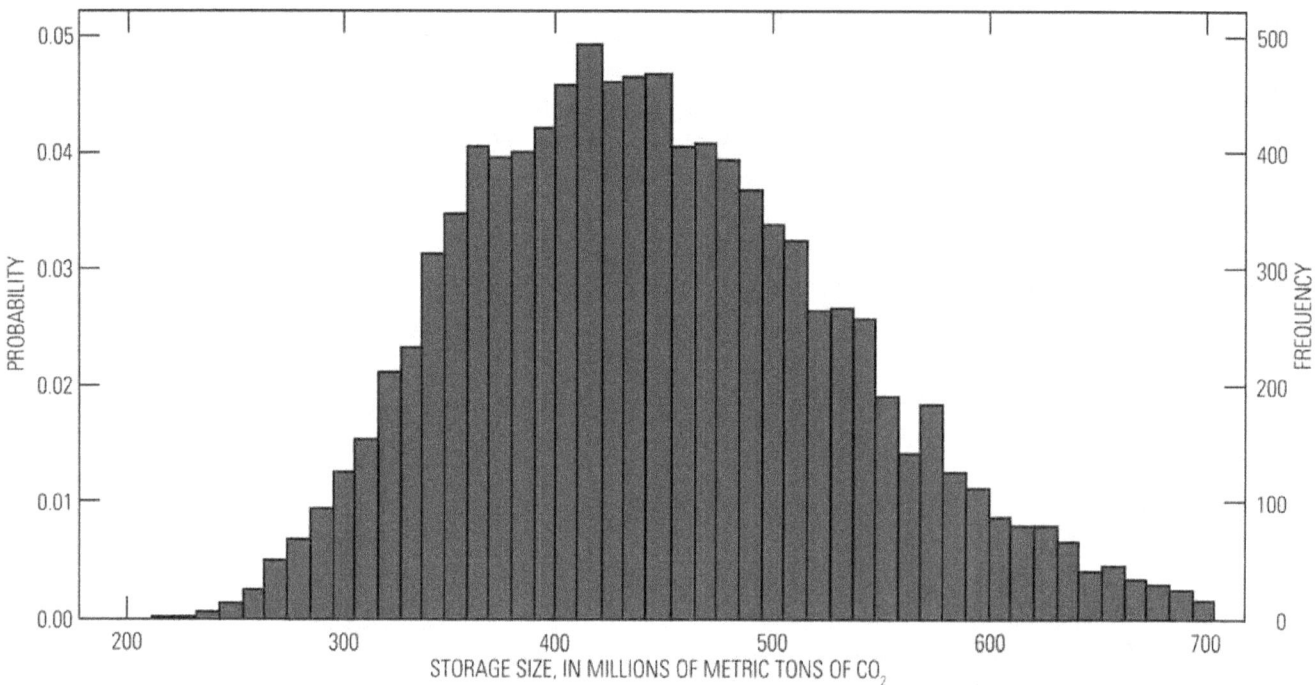

Figure 12. Probability distribution of the aggregate mass of CO_2 storage resource due to conventional EOR in 25 hypothetical oil-bearing discovered physical traps (PT_Ds) with possible storage sizes described by the distribution in figure 11.

Table 4. Percentiles of CO_2 storage resource within the distribution shown in figure 12.

Percentile	Aggregate storage, S_{EOR}, million metric tons CO_2
P95	320
P50	450
P5	630

A similar sequence of probabilistic calculations can be done for S_{NCV}. The first step is calculation of the probability distribution of possible storage size in PT_{DS} using the formula for method B in table 1. For example, NCV is calculated for PT_{DS} with cumulative production data similar to data shown in table 2. At the present stage of development of the numerical methods, we use a default value of 1.0 for C_{WD}, but a distribution of values could be determined by an assessment geologist using data from production histories of the PT_{DS}. The subsurface density of CO_2 at reservoir temperature and pressure appropriate for the SAU is calculated from the online database, "Thermophysical Properties of Fluid Systems," provided by the National Institute of Standards and Technology (2009). Because the depth of PT_{DS} can vary between 3,000 and 13,000 ft, and geothermal gradients in basins have some spatial variability, we use a distribution of CO_2 densities with a range that spans the possible minima and maxima of temperatures and pressures in the SAU. The formula for method B and distributions of NCV, C_{WD}, and ρ_{CO2} are used with Crystal Ball™ to calculate a size distribution of storage in PT_{DS}. Then the number of PT_{DS} and the calculated size distribution are used to calculate the distribution of aggregate storage resource in exactly the same manner as in the preceding example of storage resource through conventional EOR.

Calculation of S_{TKV} follows the same pattern; see method C in table 1. The only significant difference is that for traps in formations with a large range of depth and (or) thickness in the SAU, there may be several thickness intervals for which the storage resource may be calculated. For example, if the base of the SAU extends to depths greater than 13,000 ft, then storage resources can be calculated within the depth interval from 3,000 to 13,000 ft or within the full formation interval from 3,000 ft to maximum depth. If overpressure conditions exist, then the SAU interval thickness extends from the top of the formation where it is >3,000 ft deep to the depth of the top of the overpressure zone.

Following calculation of S_{TKV}, the storage resource in the total trap volume, S_{TTV}, is calculated by using a growth factor, C_G, that represents the potential increase in volume up to the spill point of the trap. See method D in table 1.

3.2.2. Probabilistic Modeling of Storage in Saline Formations

The probabilistic calculations use the inputs from uncertainty of the mean for the area, net porous interval, and porosity and the C_{SE} distribution for the SF to model the probability distribution of possible storage sizes for the SF (fig. 13). Unlike the PT method, which uses a number distribution and a size distribution to determine the storage distribution, the SF method has no number distribution, as there is only one SF for each SAU. Therefore, the storage size distribution determined by the above calculation is the distribution of CO_2 storage for the SF.

Saline Formation Calculation

Means (green) from the raw data distibution serve as the basis for the assessing geologist's determination of the upper (purple) and lower (blue) uncertainty of the mean values. These three values define triangular distributions that reflect the uncertainty that the means of the available data represent the actual mean values throughout the SF.

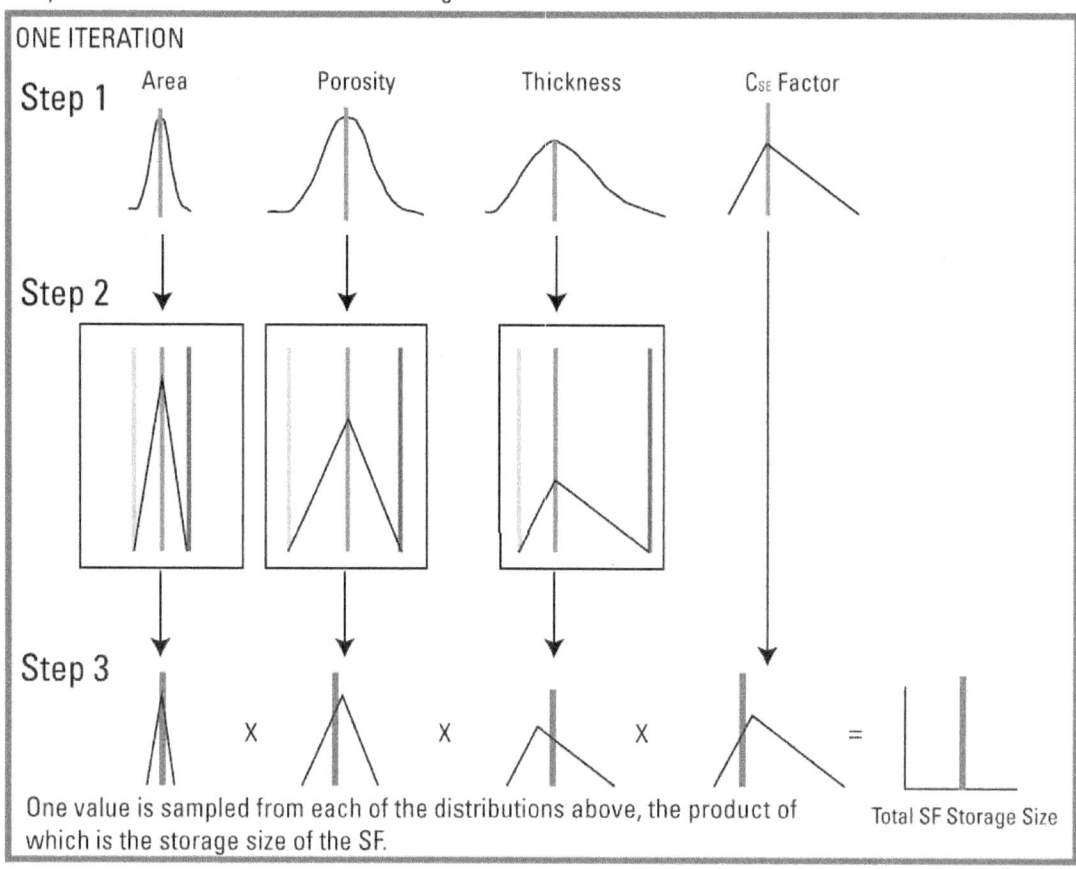

Step 4

Steps 1, 2, and 3 are repeated for each iteration. The conditional calculation, shown below, is the distribution of the aggregate storage sizes. For the unconditional calculation, the success of each iteration is assessed via the probability of containment. Iterations that are not successful are assigned values of zero, lowering the mean of the distribution of aggregate storage sizes.

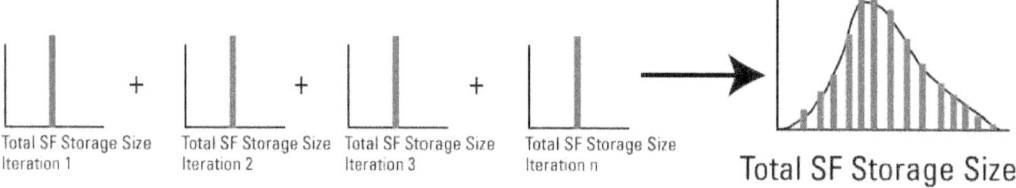

Figure 13.   A flow diagram illustrating how the aggregate saline formation (SF) storage distribution is generated from input values on the SF form (appendix A.2). C_{SE}, storage efficiency factor.

3.2.3. Assigning Geologic Probability Values to Determine Unconditional Storage Resources

The calculations in sections 3.2.1 and 3.2.2 are used to determine the conditional CO_2 storage resource, which is the amount of storage possible without assessing success. Although storage resource exists throughout the SAU in both PTs and the SF, there remains a possibility that storage within some of the PTs or the SF may not be successful. Success is defined as the probability that, on the basis of geological, geochemical, and geophysical evidence, there is a likelihood that CO_2 will be retained at volumes equal to or greater than the minimum size. For PTs, this minimum size, as described in section 2.1.4, is 12.5 MMbbl. For SFs, the minimum size is the product of the minimum storage efficiency value for that SF and its calculated pore volume. This minimum value will typically be no less than 1 percent of the total pore volume of the SF. The likelihood of success is determined by geologic factors that are not taken into account during the calculation of the conditional storage volume. These geologic factors are combined and referred to below as the geologic probability. The geologic probability, when applied to the probabilistic calculations, results in the estimation of the unconditional storage resource.

The primary factor in determining the geologic probability, which is used to evaluate the success of the individual PT or the SF, is the probability of containment. This probability of containment differs from how containment is discussed in section 2.6. The probability of containment estimates the likelihood that CO_2 will be stored within a PT or the SF above the minimum amount. If the assessment geologists have some evidence for seismic, injection, or reactivity issues, they should raise them during the assessment. However, it is difficult to numerically evaluate how these factors might reduce the potential for storage success in a PT or the SF, so values must be assigned on the basis of the judgment of the assessment geologists.

The probability of containment is some number between 0 and 1, with a 1 being a certainty of storing the minimum volume of CO_2 within an individual PT or the SF. If the value is less than 1, then it will reduce the number of PTs that meet the size limit (fig. 10). The reduced number of PTs is then used to determine the unconditional aggregate storage resource. The probability of containment for the SF captures the possibility that the CO_2 contained within the formation will not be above some minimum percentage of the total pore space (fig. 13). Therefore, if the probability of containment is less than 1, then some of the iterations of the probabilistic calculations will be zeroed, essentially assessed as no storage, as there is a chance that the SF will not meet the minimum storage requirements. This treatment is similar to the assessment-level probability of NOGA. The modified, presumably lesser, storage aggregate distribution for

PTs and storage size distribution for the SF are referred to as the unconditional storage resource as it incorporates the geologic probability that the CO_2 will be contained within the PTs or the SF.

3.3. Data Sources and Manipulations

3.3.1. Sources

Geologic and assessment models are built on geologic framework studies from USGS oil and gas assessments. Such basin studies have resulted in structure and thickness models, stratigraphic columns, cross sections, and general knowledge of the geology that are used to identify the SAU. Additional comprehensive data searches from published and unpublished work by the USGS, State geological surveys, producer associations or agencies; commercial databases; and the general literature are conducted to obtain additional information for use by assessment geologists. Quantitative data at the oil and gas field and reservoir level, including composition, porosity, permeability, size, thickness, depths, lithology, drive mechanism, and production data, are available in a commercial database, "Significant Oil and Gas Fields of the United States" (Nehring Associates, Inc., 2008). This database contains information on all fields with at least 0.5 million barrels of oil equivalent (MMBOE) known recovery (cumulative production plus reserves). Data at the individual well level, including location, producing formation, formation tops, bottom hole pressures, perforation zones, and production of oil, gas, and water, were obtained from the commercial database, "PI/Dwights PLUS on CD" (IHS Inc., 2008a). Volumes of produced and injected water, oil, gas, and condensate, along with core sample measurements, were obtained from a separate IHS database called "PIDM 2.5" (IHS Inc., 2008b).

3.3.2. Manipulations

The areas of PT_Ds were calculated with a geographic information system (GIS) procedure. Data from Nehring and IHS databases were compiled using Nehring field names. All production well locations available in the IHS database that were assigned to a field name in the SAU were plotted. A "rubber-band outline" was constructed around the wells using a 300-m (984-ft) buffer. Any wells that were assigned the same field name but that were separated by more than 3 miles from any well with the same field name were excluded from the field outline. Areas within the outline were calculated for each field. These values were summed, with overlapping field areas removed, generating the area of the PT_Ds.

Accurate calculations of the net cumulative volume of produced fluids for each PT_D require a procedure used in petroleum engineering called material balance (Craft and Hawkins, 1991). This procedure corrects all volumes of produced fluids that are measured at surface conditions to subsurface conditions. However, such calculations require detailed information about the production history and volumetric properties of fluids that is not available to the USGS. Therefore, NCV was calculated by an approximation method that allowed simple conversion of the surface volume of produced gas in thousands of cubic feet to subsurface volume in barrels. This method allowed the net cumulative volumes of gas, oil, condensate, and water to be summed and converted to subsurface pore volume. The approximation method for converting surface gas volume in thousands of cubic feet (MCF) to subsurface volume in barrels is based on the fact that the formation volume factor (FVF) for gas in the depth range of 3,000 to 13,000 ft (Schuenemeyer, 2005) ranges from 100 to 300 surface volumes per reservoir volume and that there are 5.61 cubic feet per barrel (cf/bbl). If a FVF of 178 is chosen and converted to barrels, 1 MCF at the surface is equivalent to 1 barrel of pore volume in the subsurface. This approximation nevertheless allows rapid evaluation of total fluid volumes in the subsurface. Surface volumes of oil and condensate should be corrected to subsurface volumes also, but, given the uncertainty introduced by the gas volume conversion, corrections to the oil and condensate volumes do not appear to be necessary.

3.4. Basic Input Data Forms

The purpose of the input forms is to gather all the relevant data in one spreadsheet to supply values for the probabilistic calculations and to consolidate important observations about the SAU to facilitate storage assessment discussions. The forms are based on the USGS National Oil and Gas Assessment (NOGA) input forms (Klett and others, 2005a; Klett and Schmoker, 2005). The PT assessment form is similar to that used by the NOGA conventional assessment methodology, and the SF form resembles the one used by the North Slope Alaska Deposit Model methodology. The NOGA assessment methods for both types of accumulations were important in the development of the CO_2 sequestration methodology. For example, discovered and undiscovered petroleum accumulations are assigned to geologically consistent units called assessment units (AUs) (Schmoker and Klett, 2005); similarly, storage assessment units (SAUs) are used in the CO_2 sequestration methodology. Each AU is assessed individually, and an input data form is completed for each one. Using oil and gas information, the assessment geologist estimates for each AU the probability of occurrence of at least one accumulation that has the potential to be added to petroleum reserves (Klett and Schmoker, 2005). The CO_2 methodology uses similar concepts, based on the attributes and characteristics of SAUs that are important for CO_2 sequestration.

3.4.1. Physical Trap Form

The "Physical Traps (PTs) Assessment Model: Basic Input Data Form" (appendix A.1) is derived from the NOGA conventional accumulation assessment form (Klett and others, 2005a). However, instead of consolidating data based on the production history of conventional accumulations to determine how much resource remains to be discovered, the goal of the PT input form is to gather both production and volumetric data for use in assessing the volume of CO_2 that can be stored. There are inputs for observations that describe relevant features of the SAU and PTs, as well as for the distributions of values needed for the probabilistic calculations to assess the storage resource in each of the four storage classifications for PTs. These input sections are described below, and the steps in the assessment process are shown in figure 14.

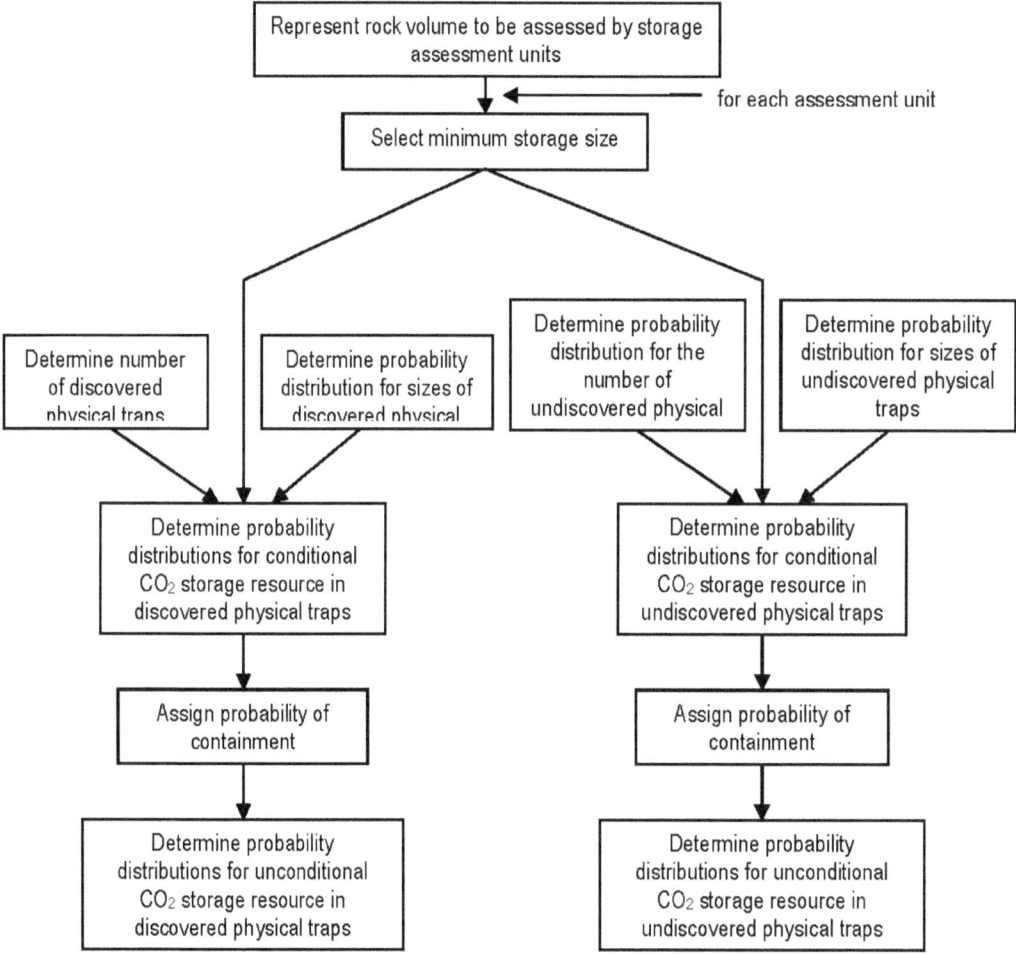

Figure 14. Flow diagram of key steps in the USGS assessment method for estimating the CO_2 storage resources in discovered and undiscovered physical traps. These steps are followed for each storage method. See text and the physical trap form (appendix A.1) for more information.

3.4.1.1. Identification Information

The initial section of the PT form includes basic identification and description of the SAU, as well as a section for notes from the assessing geologist. Lines for the assessing geologist's name and the names of the assessment region, province, and SAU are present. NOGA naming conventions will be used for the SAUs. NOGA uses a numeric code identifying each region, province, total petroleum system, and assessment unit; these codes are globally uniform and identify the same item in all publications. The codes are constructed as follows: region, single digit; province, three digits to the right of the region code; total petroleum system, two digits to the right of the province code; and assessment unit, two digits to the right of the petroleum system code. For CO_2 storage assessment, the SAU code will end in "S" to differentiate it from NOGA assessment unit codes. The SAU name should include the name of the storage formation and the name of the regional seal formation. The spatial relationship between the SAU and the NOGA assessment unit (AU) can be recorded following the SAU information. Detailed notes should go under assessors' notes at the end of the section. The next line records the date of the source material that was used to populate data fields in this form. Notes from the assessors provide details and conditions specific to the assessment unit that are pertinent for comparative and research purposes.

3.4.1.2. Characteristics of Storage Assessment Unit

The characteristics of the storage assessment unit (SAU) are entered in the second section of the form. These physical characteristics define the boundaries of the SAU and are the first step in determining SAU area. The first question refers to the range of preferred storage depths between 3,000 and 13,000 ft, as discussed in section 2.1.2. The second line records the area of the SAU defined by the depth range. The default depth cutoff for storage of 13,000 ft may be superseded by overpressure [pressure/depth (P/D) > 0.5 psi/ft] if it occurs at depths shallower than 13,000 ft. The SAU area, incorporating the possible occurrence of overpressure, is entered on Line 3a. The minimum, mode, and maximum of the total storage formation thickness, estimated according to the criteria in the questions above, are entered on the lines at the end of this section.

3.4.1.3. Numerical Inputs

The entries in the section of the form on numerical inputs determine the number of traps used to estimate the aggregate storage resource. A minimum potential storage volume is used to constrain the number of traps. This volume is based on the net cumulative volume (produced volume minus injected volume) of all fluids (oil, gas, and water) produced from the trap. In this version of the assessment methodology, the minimum volume is ~12.5 million barrels (MMbbl), which is equivalent to 2 million m^3. However, this value can be changed as needed to meet the goals of a specific assessment. The number of PT$_{DS}$ that meet or exceed this minimum size is determined and entered on the second line. The next two lines show the number of oil and gas traps determined from the gas:oil ratios (GOR). The number of PT$_{DS}$ that are oil traps, is needed to calculate the storage resource that will result from conventional CO_2 EOR.

3.4.1.4. Characteristics of Physical Traps in the Storage Assessment Unit

Data distributions for the following six factors are required to complete the storage calculations in the next section of the form. Values for original oil in place (OOIP) are available in the Nehring Associates, Inc., database (Nehring Associates, Inc., 2008) or can be calculated. Net cumulative produced volume is the volume of oil and water and gas produced minus the volume of injected water and injected gas corrected for reservoir conditions. The result is a net cumulative production that indicates the amount of material that occupied pore space in the subsurface that has been removed. Area on Line 10 is defined as the surficial area of the PT$_D$ fields, as delineated by wells that have produced. The net porous interval represents the thickness of the formation that contains a porous constituent, not formation thickness. Porosity data for the PT$_{DS}$ are taken from Nehring Associates database (Nehring Associates, Inc., 2008) and IHS (IHS Inc., 2008b). The storage efficiency factor, or C_{SE}, is a distribution that defines the fraction of the total available pore space that will be occupied by free-phase CO_2.

3.4.1.5. Storage Volume Calculation Methods

Four different storage volume calculation methods (A–D) are included in the PT assessment form and in table 1. Generally, the storage capacities will increase from method A to method D as they become more heavily based on estimates of the volumetric properties of the PT$_D$ than on measured volumes of produced fluids. Data for PT$_{US}$ can be determined using an internal analog based on size and number distributions from the NOGA assessments of undiscovered fields.

In method A, the storage resource is based on engineering experience with present-day CO_2 enhanced-oil-recovery (EOR) methods. The equations for calculating storage due to EOR are included in the form. This method yields the most conservative estimate of sequestration storage volume.

Method B is based on the net cumulative volume (NCV) of produced fluids. This method of determining pore space is based on volumes of hydrocarbon and water production and injection as discussed in section 3.4.1.4.

Method C, total known volume (TKV), uses the volumetric properties of the trap, area, net porous interval, porosity, and the storage efficiency factor to estimate the available pore space within the PT_D.

The final classification, method D, is based on the total trap volume to the spill point (TTV). The TKV storage volume calculated with method C is increased by a growth factor (C_G) to yield the TTV. The productive area that defines the PT_D does not necessarily represent the area of the PT to the spill point. C_G is determined by the assessor to represent the increase in storage volume that would result if the field outline were extended to the trap's spill point. The growth factor allows for an approximation of the resulting increase in area to be factored into the storage volume calculation. However, this C_G factor can only be determined by the assessment geologist if relevant data exist.

3.4.1.6. Physical Trap Probability of Containment

Probability of containment is the fraction of traps that will be able to contain a volume of at least 12.5 MMbbl (2 million m^3) CO_2 as discussed in section 3.2.3. This value will modify the number of traps considered in the calculation of the aggregate storage resources.

3.4.1.7. Selected Ancillary Data

The selected ancillary data section will aid the assessing geologist in determining the probability of containment value. Of equal importance, this section records any factors that will have a significant effect on CO_2 sequestration success. The assessing geologist is expected to provide, as additional information to the assessment team, descriptions of any physical, chemical, and mineralogical characteristics of the reservoir and confining layers that may have a negative effect on sequestration. The following descriptions of the various inputs in the ancillary data section provide the necessary context required by the assessing geologist to complete this section of the form.

Injectivity is indicated by the ability of the CO_2 pumped into the subsurface to enter the storage formation and move away from the injection point. Transmissivity (see glossary) may be a major factor for estimating injectivity.

Depth to top of storage has implications for the confining potential of the seal and storage formation. In addition, the depth converted to subsurface pressure and temperature can be used to estimate the density of CO_2 needed to convert storage volume to storage mass. The confining layer acts both as a seal and as a potential sink for formation water. Confining-layer characteristics that might affect the probability of containment must be taken into account by the assessing geologist. Natural seismic risk, which is estimated from the historic seismicity of the region, can raise containment concerns. Whether currently active or not, a seismic zone may provide conduits within the storage formation where CO_2 could bypass the seal formation.

Variations in reservoir architecture will be important for estimates of injectivity. For example, a homogeneous massive sand body may have the same volume as a group of many thin, discontinuous heterogeneous sand bodies, but injecting into the latter may be limited by the architecture of the sand body. The drive mechanism for the field provides an indication of the flow properties of the storage unit, particularly the potential for displacement of water from the formation and the ability to inject CO_2. Description of the drive mechanism may not be available but may be inferred by the assessment geologist from production data.

Geochemical reactivity is discussed in section 2.5. Fluid rock reactions can increase or decrease porosity and permeability of the storage formation, thereby affecting injectivity. Geologic age and knowledge of the extent of diagenesis may also contribute important information to studies of reactivity in the storage formation.

Information on formation water composition, mineral composition, and CO_2-brine-mineral interactions at specific temperature and pressure conditions are to be documented in the ancillary data. All affect reactivity and the possible outcomes of geochemical interactions.

3.4.1.8. Allocations of Physical Traps

The final section of the form covers the allocation of CO_2 storage volume by area for Federal, State, tribal, and private lands and NOGA provinces. Allocations include areas such as wilderness areas, national forests, national parks, and political areas, such as State and county land. The allocation is based on ownership of surface and (or) mineral rights. Owing to the nature of the storage resource distributions per allocation, the total of these allocations does not necessarily equal the total storage volume calculated in the assessment.

3.4.2. Saline Formation Form

The SF form (appendix A.2) is created to aggregate the data needed to assess the volume of CO_2 that can be stored within the SF on a purely volumetric basis. As in the PT form, the SF form has inputs for the observations that describe relevant features about the SAU and SF. Input for the range and distribution of values of volumetric parameters are needed for the probabilistic equations to calculate the distribution of possible storage resources in the SF. The process for completing these calculations is depicted in figure 15.

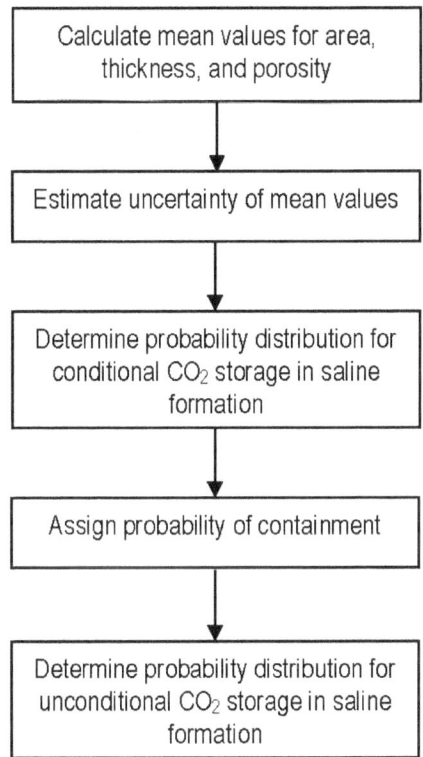

Figure 15. Flow diagram of key steps in the USGS assessment method for estimating the CO_2 storage resources in saline formations. See text and saline formation form (appendix A.2) for more information.

3.4.2.1. Identification Information

The sections on identification information are the same on the PT form and the SF form. See text section 3.4.1.1.

3.4.2.2. Characteristics of Storage Assessment Unit

The sections on SAU characteristics are the same on the PT form and the SF form. See text section 3.4.1.2.

3.4.2.3. Area Calculation for the Saline Formation

Subtracting the area of the PT_{DS} and the PT_{US} from the total SAU area yields a range of the areas of the SF outside of traps. The PT form documents the sum of areas for PT_{DS} greater than the minimum size. The distribution and average of the area of the PT_{US} greater than the minimum size can be provided by the NOGA team with values modified using the published assessment reports and the area distribution of the PT_{DS}. Fields smaller than the minimum storage size are included in the area of the SF.

3.4.2.4. Characteristics of the Saline Formation

The net porous interval represents the thickness of the formation that contains a porous constituent; this value is not total formation thickness. When the assessment geologist is determining the mean porosity value for the SF and the uncertainty of that mean, the porosity data from fields that were not included in the PT assessment should carry a greater weight than the porosity data from fields that were included in the PT assessment. The relative robustness or paucity of the datasets for the area, thickness, and porosity will be the main control on the uncertainty that the assessing geologist applies to the calculated mean values.

Storage efficiency (C_{SE}) is the fraction of the total available pore space that will be occupied by free-phase CO_2. The distribution of storage efficiency values must be justified by the assessment geologist; see section 2.6 for discussion of issues related to the estimation of the storage efficiency factor.

3.4.2.5. Saline Formation Storage Volume

The storage volume represents the pore volume for the entire SF. The volume is the product of a probabilistic calculation that samples the distributions of uncertainty about the mean of the area, net porous interval thickness, and porosity. The calculation includes the distribution of possible storage efficiency factors. These inputs are recorded on the form.

3.4.2.6. Saline Formation Probability of Containment

Text section 3.4.1.6 addresses the use of probability of containment for the four PT storage calculations. In the case of the SF assessment, the discussion of probabilities is equally relevant.

3.4.2.7. Selected Ancillary Data

Text section 3.4.1.7 about the PT form discusses the same ancillary data inputs that are requested on the SF form.

3.4.2.8. Allocations of the Saline Formation

The sections on allocation are the same on the PT form and the SF form. See text section 3.4.1.8.

4. Discussion: Science and Data Needs

The science and data needs discussed in this section are specific to development of assessment methodologies for CO_2 resources. There are many other science and engineering issues that are specific to the deployment of large-scale CO_2 storage projects. However, many of those issues are site specific and are not within the scope of this methodology. The issues we discuss below will help to reduce the uncertainty of subsequent national assessments of resources for geologic storage of CO_2.

Of particular importance will be new information from large-scale demonstration projects on geologic storage of CO_2. Seven projects are currently funded by DOE within their Regional Carbon Sequestration Partnership program (U.S. Department of Energy, 2009). As more information on the performance of CO_2 injection and storage projects, including large scale CO_2 EOR projects, becomes available, we will be able to refine assessment methods for CO_2 storage by incorporating experience from the in-place behavior of injected CO_2. Future assessment methodologies will benefit as these data become available and can be incorporated.

4.1. Inputs for Probabilistic Calculations

Though there is an attempt to estimate the storage efficiency of PTs and SFs in this methodology, there are no analogs at present to evaluate these values. There have been attempts at modeling these values (van der Meer, 1995) or calculating them with probabilistic methods (U.S. Department of Energy, National Energy Technology Laboratory, 2008a). The factors that are important for determining storage efficiency, such as containment, injectivity, and reactivity, are understood on a basic level from laboratory experiments, computer models, and very small scale injection projects (Hovorka and others, 2004). However, there are few analogs for large-scale CO_2 storage projects in SFs [for example, Sleipner (Arts and others, 2008)] or PTs [for example, Weyburn (Emberley and others, 2005) and In Salah (Riddiford and others, 2005)] to evaluate these experiments, models, or calculations. When the results of planned large-scale CO_2 storage projects are available, they should provide the observations and measurements that will refine estimates of storage efficiency factors.

4.2. Aggregation of Storage Volumes at the Basin and National Level

This methodology is designed to estimate the distribution of CO_2 storage resource in individual SAUs. To provide information and decision support to policy makers at a variety of scales that may range from an individual State or specific Federal lands to total storage in the nation, we need methods to combine (aggregate) resources of multiple SAUs and multiple regions into single distributions of the quantity of storage. To properly define the distribution of uncertainty about the mean of the aggregate resource, we must account for statistical dependencies of volumetric parameters between SAUs within a single geologic province or among provinces. Additional work is needed to develop statistical algorithms that can account for dependencies and properly aggregate storage resources as needed for policy makers

4.3. Geochemistry

Better knowledge of CO_2-water-rock interactions at in-place pressures, depths, and formation water compositions in large-scale demonstration projects (for example, projects of the DOE Regional Carbon Sequestration Partnerships) will be important for evaluating the effects of geochemical reactions on the storage of CO_2. In-place studies to date are limited in number and size (for example, Kharaka and others, 2006), and most prior work has been laboratory experiments or computer modeling using reactive transport codes.

To fully understand the potential impact of formation water displacement by CO_2 injection and storage, we need baseline information on formation water chemistry, including naturally occurring concentrations of components that may be considered environmental contaminants. Although data from the petroleum industry are available in the USGS produced-waters database (Breit, 2002) the analyses are limited in quality and scope. An inventory of ground-water-quality data from 3,000 to 13,000 ft deep across the United States needs to be performed to identify available water analyses and, more importantly, to identify gaps in measurements of components that may affect ground water quality and the near-surface environment.

4.4. Seals

In addition to providing containment of buoyant CO_2, seals may be important in the uptake of formation water displaced by CO_2 injection. However, the properties that control potential storage of formation water within seals are not well understood. Furthermore, while seal properties are well understood at the PT level, there is less knowledge about the seals in a regional sense, for example, over the entire SAU. Knowledge of regional seal properties is particularly important for determining the storage efficiency of SFs. Although seal integrity in PTs can be inferred from the presence of hydrocarbons, there are no well defined criteria to identify the integrity of seals to retain buoyant CO_2 where hydrocarbons are not present.

4.5. Geologic Databases

National assessments of resource for geologic storage of CO_2 require a basic set of spatially distributed digital data. Examples include but are not limited to maps and data on geologic structure, fault locations, formation thickness, water quality, and petroleum production. Some data are currently available in the public domain. For example, the U.S. Department of Energy, National Energy Technology Laboratory (2008b), has created the NatCarb online database (*http://www.natcarb.org/*) with information available from the Federal Government, State geological surveys, and State oil and gas regulatory agencies. However, national assessments of storage resource will require access to large commercial and proprietary databases that contain detailed information on oil and gas exploration and production activities. In addition, regional evaluation of subsurface rock and fluid properties will be facilitated by access to privately owned datasets such as two and three-dimensional seismic surveys and detailed well test data. Development of data-sharing agreements between public and private organizations should be initiated to refine future assessments of storage resources.

4.6. Hydraulics and Flow

Pressure increases from CO_2 injection should propagate away from the injection site, potentially extending to and having some effect on flow boundaries (faults, unconformities, basin margins, or the updip extent or depth limit of the storage formation). Potential hazards from large-scale CO_2 injection could be induced seismicity, contamination of shallow ground water, and transport of contaminants out of the storage formation. Flow of buoyant fluids such as CO_2, particularly in fractures and low-permeability rock, also needs further investigation. Movement of CO_2 and estimated CO_2 plume velocities are important factors in determining the areal extent of the CO_2 plume and the volume of rock that the plume contacts. Understanding the movement and effects of CO_2 injection will provide more accurate storage efficiencies and assessment volumes.

4.7. Injectivity

Injectivity is a rate-based parameter that characterizes the ability of CO_2 to enter a storage formation. For geological assessments of storage resources, it should be defined by rock and fluid properties and subsurface pressure, not by engineering and economic parameters (number of wells, injection pressure, etc). At this stage of development of our probabilistic methodology, we are unable to clearly distinguish geologic parameters from engineering and economic factors. However, on a qualitative basis, it is evident that variations in injectivity will significantly impact estimates of storage resources, particularly in assessments of resources that are available within a fixed time span (that is projects with decadal lifetimes of injection).

We believe an important next step in development of assessment methodology will be a clear definition of injectivity that can be quantified and incorporated in probabilistic calculations.

5. Conclusions

The goal of this report is to describe a new methodology that uses a probabilistic model that aids in assessing the CO_2 storage resource of geologic strata in different geologic settings. Creating the methodology involved the combination of (1) the knowledge of hydrology, the fluid flow of both aqueous and buoyant fluids, geochemistry, petrophysics, and other geologic evidence; (2) USGS experience with the assessment of petroleum resources; and (3) extensive datasets, both proprietary and nonproprietary, which the USGS has compiled on the rock, fluid, and production properties of the storage and seal formations of the storage assessment units (SAUs). This methodology treats the physical traps (PTs) and the saline formation (SF) as endmembers of a combined system, which allows for the most comprehensive assessment that the USGS can conduct on a given SAU. The goal of the methodology was also to provide the resource assessment in several parts, so that decisionmakers can assess various classifications of storage in the SAUs. The PTs are subdivided into resource assessments on basis of the storage potential due to (1) enhanced oil recovery, (2) the net produced volume of fluid, and (3) the volumetrics of the geologic strata. These classifications and the volumetric assessment of SFs are also reported as conditional volumes (that is, reported without taking into account the geologic probabilities) and as unconditional volumes, which are reduced by incorporating the geologic probabilities. The breadth of the methodology, both in the scope of what it accounts for and the wide range of results it can produce, should provide decisionmakers and stakeholders with a wealth of information to develop informed conclusions.

Acknowledgments

The authors gratefully and enthusiastically thank Ronald R. Charpentier (USGS) for expert guidance and advice on developing probabilistic models and calculations. Christopher P. Garrity (USGS) created much-needed GIS algorithms to define field areas in physical traps. In the methodology development process, extensive collaboration was provided by the USGS Tertiary assessment team, especially Alexander W. Karlsen, and the USGS Wind River Basin Province assessment team, in particular Mark Kirschbaum and Laura Roberts. James J. Thordsen (USGS) contributed data for hydrologic analysis. Susan D. Hovorka and the Gulf Coast Carbon Center team at the Texas Bureau of Economic Geology provided data and helpful discussions on the potential for CO_2 storage in the sediments of the Texas Gulf Coast. The authors appreciate support from Richard Nehring (Nehring Associates, Inc.). Kathleen Winner and Jeffrey S. Kay (IHS, Inc.) gave permission to publish production data. The content and presentation of this report benefited greatly from the technical reviews of Scott Frailey (Illinois State Geological Survey) and USGS scientists David W. Houseknecht, Ronald R. Charpentier, and James L. Coleman. The authors thank Desiree Polyak (USGS) for her contributions to the project. Eric Morrissey (USGS) was helpful in the redesign of several illustrations within the report. The authors also wish to acknowledge the support of the USGS Enterprise Publishing Network, specifically Elizabeth Good and Anna Glover, and the Eastern Region Geology Discipline Bureau Approving Official Kathie Rankin.

References Cited

Arts, R., Chadwick, A., Eiken, O., Thibeau, S., and Nooner, S., 2008, Ten years' experience of monitoring CO_2 injection in the Utsira Sand at Sleipner, offshore Norway: First Break, v. 26, p. 65–73.

Bachu, S., 2003, Screening and ranking of sedimentary basins for sequestration of CO_2 in geological media in response to climate change: Environmental Geology, v. 44, p. 277–289.

Bachu, S., Bonijoly, D., Bradshaw, J., Burruss, R., Holloway, S., Christensen, N.P., and Mathiassen, O.M., 2007, CO_2 storage capacity estimation—Methodology and gaps: International Journal of Greenhouse Gas Control, v. 1, p. 430–443.

Beaumont, E.A., and Fielder, F., 2000, Formation fluid pressure and its application, in chap. 5 of Beaumont E.A., and Foster, N.H., eds., Treatise of Petroleum Geology, Handbook of Petroleum Geology: Exploring for Oil and Gas Traps: Tulsa, Okla., American Association of Petroleum Geologists, p. 5.1–5.64.

Benson, Sally, and Cook, Peter, 2005, Underground geological storage, chap. 5 of Intergovernmental Panel on Climate Change (IPCC), Working Group III, IPCC special report on carbon dioxide capture and storage (Metz, Bert, Davidson, Ogunlade, de Coninck, Heleen, Loos, Manuela, and Meyer, Leo, eds.): New York, Cambridge University Press, p. 195–276. (Also available online *http://www.ipcc.ch/ipccreports/srccs.htm.*) (Accessed January 13, 2009.)

Bradshaw, John, 2004, Geological sequestration of CO_2; Why, where and what role for geoscientists [abs.], *in* Boult, P.J., Johns, D.R., and Lang, S.C., eds., Eastern Australasian Basins Symposium II, 19–22d September 2004, Adelaide, South Australia [conference proceedings]: Sydney, Australia, Petroleum Exploration Society of Australia, p. 737.

Bradshaw, J., Bachu, S., Bonijoly, D., Burruss, R., Holloway, S., Christensen, N.P., and Mathiassen, O.M., 2007, CO_2 storage capacity estimation—Issues and development of standards: International Journal of Greenhouse Gas Control, v. 1, p. 62–68.

Breit, G.N., comp., 2002, Produced waters database: U.S. Geological Survey database available online at *http://energy.cr.usgs.gov/prov/prodwat/index.htm.* (Accessed January 14, 2009.)

Brennan, S.T., and Burruss, R.C., 2006, Specific storage volumes—A useful tool for CO_2 storage capacity assessment: Natural Resources Research, v. 15, no. 3, p. 165–182, doi:10.1007/s11053–006–9019–0.

Brennan, S.T., Dennen, K.O., and Burruss, R.C., 2006, Timing of hydrocarbon emplacement in ozokerite and calcite lined fractures, Teapot Dome, Wyoming: U.S. Geological Survey Open-File Report 2006–1214, 23 p., available online at *http://egsc.usgs.gov/isb/pubs/ofrs/2006-1214/OFR2006-1214.pdf.* (Accessed January 15, 2009.)

Brown, Alton, 2003, Capillary effects on fault-fill sealing: American Association of Petroleum Geologists Bulletin, v. 87, no. 3, p. 381–395

Buckley, Glen, Ritchie, Earl, Stanton, Bill, and Kumar, Naresh, 1999, Report [of the] American Association of Petroleum Geologists Committee on Resource Evaluation (CORE) Subcommittee to Review the World Assessment Methodology used by the USGS: [Tulsa, Okla.,] American Association of Petroleum Geologists, 9 p., available online at *http://energy.cr.usgs.gov/oilgas/noga/methodology.html* under "Assessment Methodology—Conventional Resources, Peer Review Report." (Accessed January 13, 2009.)

Cavanagh, A.J., Wilkinsin, M., and Haszeldine, S., 2006, CO_2 sequestration site performance; Processes of storage seal failure and overburden migration: Eos Transactions, American Geophysical Union, v. 87, no. 52, suppl. 26.

Charpentier, R.R., and Klett, T.R., 2005, A Monte Carlo simulation method for the assessment of undiscovered, conventional oil and gas, chap. 21 *of* USGS Southwestern Wyoming Province Assessment Team, National Assessment of Oil and Gas Project; Petroleum systems and geologic assessment of oil and gas in the Southwestern Wyoming Province, Wyoming, Colorado, and Utah: U.S. Geological Survey Digital Data Series 69–D, 5 p., on CD–ROM. (Also available online at *http://pubs.usgs.gov/dds/dds-069/dds-069-d/.*) (Accessed January 14, 2009.)

Couples, G.D., 2005, Seals; The role of geomechanics, *in* Boult, Peter, and Kaldi, John, eds., Evaluating fault and cap rock seals: American Association of Petroleum Geologists Hedberg Series, no. 2, p. 87–108.

Craft, B.C., and Hawkins, M.F, 1991, Applied petroleum reservoir engineering (2^d ed., revised by R.E. Terry): Englewood Cliffs, N.J., Prentice Hall, 431 p.

Crovelli, R.A., 2005, Analytic resource assessment method for continuous petroleum accumulations—the ACCESS assessment method, chap. 22 *of* USGS Southwestern Wyoming Province Assessment Team, National Assessment of Oil and Gas Project, Petroleum systems and geologic assessment of oil and gas in the Southwestern Wyoming Province, Wyoming, Colorado and Utah: U.S. Geological Survey Digital Data Series 69–D, 7 p., on CD–ROM. (Also available online at *http://pubs.usgs.gov/dds/dds-069/dds-069-d/*.) (Accessed January 14, 2009.)

Curtis, John, Kumar, Naresh, Ray, Pulak, Riese, Rusty, and Ritter, John, 2001, Report [of the] American Association of Petroleum Geologists Committee on Resource Evaluation (CORE) Subcommittee to Review the United States Onshore Continuous (Unconventional) Gas Assessment Methodology Used by the USGS: [Tulsa, Okla.,] American Association of Petroleum Geologists, 20 p., available online at *http://www.aapg.org/committees/resource_evaluation/core_report.pdf.* (Also available online at *http://certmapper.cr.usgs.gov/data/noga00/natl/text/core_report.pdf.*) (Accessed January 13, 2009.)

Doughty, Christine, Freifeld, B.M., and Trautz, R.C., 2007, Site characterization for CO_2 geologic storage and vice versa—The Frio brine pilot, Texas, USA as a case study: Environmental Geology, v. 54, no. 8, p. 1635–1656, doi:10.1007/s00254–007–0942–0.

Drew, L.J., 1990, Oil and gas forecasting; Reflections of a petroleum geologist: New York, Oxford University Press, 252 p.

Drew, L.J., 1997, Undiscovered petroleum and mineral resources—Assessment and controversy: New York, Plenum Press, 210 p.

Drew, L.J., and Schuenemeyer, J.H., 1993, The evolution and use of discovery process models at the U.S. Geological Survey: American Association of Petroleum Geologists Bulletin, v. 77, no. 3, p. 467–478.

Duan, Zhenhao, and Sun, Rui, 2003, An improved model calculating CO_2 solubility in pure water and aqueous NaCl solutions from 273 to 533 K and from 0 to 2000 bar: Chemical Geology, v. 193, no. 3–4, p. 257–271, doi:10.1016/S0009–2541(02)00263–2.

Emberley, S., Hutcheon, I., Shevalier, M., Durocher, K., Mayer, B., Gunter, W.D., and Perkins, E.H., 2005, Monitoring of fluid-rock interaction and CO_2 storage through produced fluid sampling at the Weyburn CO_2-injection enhanced oil recovery site, Saskatchewan, Canada: Applied Geochemistry, v. 20, no. 6, p. 1131-1157, doi:10.1016/j.apgeochem.2005.02.007.

Gluyas, J.G., and Swarbrick, R.E., 2004, Petroleum Geoscience: Boston, Blackwell Publishing, 359 p.

Gunter, W.D., Wiwehar, B., and Perkins, E.H., 1997, Aquifer disposal of CO_2-rich greenhouse gases—Extension of the time scale of experiment for CO_2-sequestering reactions by geochemical modelling: Mineralogy and Petrology, v. 59, no. 1–2, p. 121–140, doi:10.1007/BF01163065.

Han, W.S., 2008, Evaluation of CO_2 trapping mechanisms at the SACROC northern platform: site of 35 years of CO_2 injection: Socorro, N. Mex., New Mexico Institute of Mining and Technology, unpub. Ph.D. dissertation, 426 p.

Han, W.S., and McPherson, Brian, 2008, Comparison of two different equations of state for application of carbon dioxide sequestration: Advances in Water Resources, v. 31, no. 6, p. 877–890, doi:10.1016/j.advwatres.2008.01.011

Hellevang, Helge, Aagaard, Per, Oelkers, E.H., and Kvamme, Bjorn, 2005, Can dawsonite permanently trap CO_2? Environmental Science & Technology, v. 39, no. 21, p. 8281–8287, doi:10.1021/es0504791.

Hepple, R.P., and Benson, S.M., 2005, Geologic storage of carbon dioxide as a climate change mitigation strategy; Performance requirements and the implications of surface seepage: Environmental Geology, v. 47, no. 4, p. 576–585, doi:10.1007/s00254–004–1181–2.

Hermanrud, Christian, Nordgård Bolås, H.M., and Tiege, G.M.G., 2005, Seal failure related to basin-scale processes, *in* Boult, Peter, and Kaldi, John, eds., Evaluating fault and cap rock seals: American Association of Petroleum Geologists Hedberg Series, no. 2, p. 13–22.

Hitchon, B., ed., 1996, Aquifer disposal of carbon dioxide: Sherwood Park, Alberta, Canada, Geoscience Publishing Ltd., 165 p.

Houghton, J.C., Dolton, G.L., Mast, R.F., Masters, C.D., and Root, D.H., 1993, U.S. Geological Survey estimation procedure for accumulation size distributions by play: American Association of Petroleum Geologists Bulletin v. 77, no. 3, p. 454–466.

Hovorka, S.D., Doughty, Christine, Benson, S.M., Pruess, Karsten, and Knox, P.R., 2004, The impact of geological heterogeneity on CO_2 storage in brine formations—A case study from the Texas Gulf Coast: Geological Society (of London) Special Publications, v. 233, p. 147–163.

IHS Inc., 2008a, PI/Dwights PLUS on CD, v. 18, issue 7–8: Englewood, Colo., IHS Inc.

IHS Inc., 2008b, PIDM 2.5: Englewood, Colo., IHS Inc.

Jones, R.M., and Hillis, R.R., 2003, An integrated, quantitative approach to assessing fault-seal risk: American Association of Petroleum Geologists Bulletin, v. 87, no. 3, p. 507–524.

Kharaka, Y.K., Cole, D.R., Hovorka, S.D., Gunter, W.D., Knauss, K.G., and Freifeld, B.M., 2006, Gas-water-rock interactions in Frio Formation following CO_2 injection; Implications for the storage of greenhouse gases in sedimentary basins: Geology, v. 34, no. 7, p. 577–580, doi:10.1130/G22357.1.

Kharaka, Y.K., and Hanor, J.S., 2007, Deep fluids in the continents: I. Sedimentary Basins, *in* Drever, J.I.,ed., Surface and ground water, weathering and soils, treatise on geochemistry: Oxford, United Kingdom, Elsevier Ltd., v. 5, p. 1–48.

Kharaka, Y.K., Thordsen, J.J., Hovorka, S.D., Nance, S.H., Cole, D.R., Phelps, T.J., and Knauss, G.K., 2009, Potential environmental issues of CO_2 storage in deep saline aquifers—Geochemical results from the Frio-I Brine Pilot test, Texas, USA: Applied Geochemistry. In press.

Klett, T.R., Charpentier, R.R., and Schmoker, J.W., 2000, Assessment operational procedures, chap. OP *of* USGS World Energy Assessment Team, U.S. Geological Survey world petroleum assessment 2000–Description and results: U.S. Geological Survey Digital Data Series 60, 25 p., on CD–ROM. (Also available online at *http://energy.cr.usgs.gov/WEcont/chaps/OP.pdf.*) (Accessed January 14, 2009.)

Klett, T.R., and Schmoker, J.W., 2005, U.S. Geological Survey input-data form and operational procedure for the assessment of continuous petroleum accumulations, 2002, chap. 18 *of* USGS Southwestern Wyoming Province Assessment Team, National Assessment of Oil and Gas Project; Petroleum systems and geologic assessment of oil and gas in the Southwestern Wyoming Province, Wyoming, Colorado, and Utah: U.S. Geological Survey Digital Data Series 69–D, 8 p., on CD–ROM. (Also available online at *http://pubs.usgs.gov/dds/dds-069/dds-069-d/.*) (Accessed January 14, 2009.)

Klett, T.R., Schmoker, J.W., and Charpentier, R.R., 2005a, U.S. Geological Survey input-data form and operational procedure for the assessment of conventional petroleum accumulations, chap. 20 *of* USGS Southwestern Wyoming Province Assessment Team, National Assessment of Oil and Gas Project; Petroleum systems and geologic assessment of oil and gas in the Southwestern Wyoming Province, Wyoming, Colorado, and Utah: U.S. Geological Survey Digital Data Series 69–D, 7 p., on CD–ROM. (Also available online at *http://pubs.usgs.gov/dds/dds-069/dds-069-d/.*) (Accessed January 14, 2009.)

Klett, T.R., Schmoker, J.W., Charpentier, R.R., Ahlbrandt, T.S., and Ulmishek, G.Fr., 2005b, Glossary, chap. 25 *of* USGS Southwestern Wyoming Province Assessment Team, National Assessment of Oil and Gas Project; Petroleum systems and geologic assessment of oil and gas in the Southwestern Wyoming Province, Wyoming, Colorado, and Utah: U.S. Geological Survey Digital Data Series 69–D, 3 p., on CD–ROM. (Also available online at *http://pubs.usgs.gov/dds/dds-069/dds-069-d/.*) (Accessed January 14, 2009.)

Knauss, K.G., Johnson, J.W., and Steefel, C.I., 2005, Evaluation of the impact of CO_2, co-contaminant gas, aqueous fluid and reservoir rock interactions on the geologic sequestration of CO_2: Chemical Geology, v. 217, no. 3–4, p. 339–350, doi:10.1016/j.chemgeo.2004.12.017.

Lowry, D.C., 2005, Economic evaluation of prospects with a top seal risk, *in* Boult, Peter, and Kaldi, John, eds., Evaluating fault and cap rock seals: American Association of Petroleum Geologists Hedberg Series, no. 2, p. 261–268.

National Institute of Standards, 2009, Thermophysical properties of fluid systems models: NIST standard reference database number 69, available online at *http://webbook.nist.gov/chemistry/*. (Accessed January 13, 2009.)

Nehring Associates, Inc., 2008, Significant oil and gas fields of the United States database [includes data current as of December 31, 2006]: Colorado Springs, Colo., Nehring Associates, Inc.

Nordgård Bolås, H.M., Hermanrud, C., and Tiege, G.M.G., 2005, The influence of stress regimes on hydrocarbon leakage, *in* Boult, Peter, and Kaldi, John, eds., Evaluating fault and cap rock seals: American Association of Petroleum Geologists Hedberg Series, no. 2, p. 109–123.

Pacala, S., and Socolow, R., 2004, Stabilization wedges—Solving the climate problem for the next 50 years with current technologies: Science, v. 305, no. 5686, p. 968–972, doi:10.1126/science.1100103.

Palandri, J.L., Rosenbauer, R.J., and Kharaka, Y.K., 2005, Ferric iron in sediments as a novel CO_2 mineral trap; CO_2–SO_2 reaction with hematite: Applied Geochemistry, v. 20, no. 11, p. 2038–2048, doi:10.1016/j.apgeochem.2005.06.005.

Perry, T.D., IV, Cygan, R.T., and Mitchell, Ralph, 2007, Molecular models of a hydrated calcite mineral surface: Geochimica et Cosmochimica Acta, v. 71, no. 24, p. 5876–5887, doi:10.1016/j.gca.2007.08.030.

Public Law 110–140, 2007, Energy Independence and Security Act of 2007, U.S. Government Printing Office, available online at *http://frwebgate.access.gpo.gov/cgi-bin/getdoc.cgi?dbname=110_cong_public_laws&docid=f:publ140.110.pdf*. (Accessed January 14, 2009.

Riddiford, Fred, Wright, Iain, Bishop, Clive, Espie, Tony, and Tourqui, A., 2005, Monitoring geological storage in the In Salah gas CO_2 storage project, *in* Wilson, M., Morris, T., Gale, J., and Thambimuthu, K., eds., Papers and panel discussion, v. 2, part 1 *of* Greenhouse gas control technologies—Proceedings of the 7th International Conference on Greenhouse Gas Control Technologies: Amsterdam, Elsevier, p. 1353–1359.

Rosenbauer, R.J., Koksalan, T., and Palandri, J.L., 2005, Experimental investigation of CO_2-brine-rock interactions at elevated temperature and pressure—Implications for CO_2 sequestration in deep-saline aquifers: Fuel Processing Technology, v. 86, p. 1581–1597.

Schmoker, J.W., 2005, U.S. Geological Survey assessment concepts for continuous petroleum accumulations, chap. 13 *of* USGS Southwestern Wyoming Province Assessment Team, National Assessment of Oil and Gas Project; Petroleum systems and geologic assessment of oil and gas in the Southwestern Wyoming Province, Wyoming, Colorado, and Utah: U.S. Geological Survey Digital Data Series 69–D, 7 p., on CD–ROM. (Also available online at *http://pubs.usgs.gov/dds/dds-069/dds-069-d/.*)

Schmoker, J.W., and Klett, T.R., 2000, U.S. Geological Survey assessment model for undiscovered conventional oil, gas, and NGL resources; The seventh approximation, chap. AM. *of* USGS World Energy Assessment Team, U.S. Geological Survey world petroleum assessment 2000—Description and results: U.S. Geological Survey Digital Data Series 60, 18 p., on CD–ROM. (Also available online at *http://energy.cr.usgs.gov/WEcont/chaps/AM.pdf.*) (Accessed January 14, 2009.)

Schmoker, J.W., and Klett, T.R., 2005, U.S. Geological Survey assessment concepts for conventional petroleum accumulations, chap. 19 *of* USGS Southwestern Wyoming Province Assessment Team, National Assessment of Oil and Gas Project; Petroleum systems and geologic assessment of oil and gas in the Southwestern Wyoming Province, Wyoming, Colorado, and Utah: U.S. Geological Survey Digital Data Series 69–D, 6 p., on CD–ROM. (Also available online at *http://pubs.usgs.gov/dds/dds-069/dds-069-d/.*)

Schuenemeyer, J.H., 2005, Methodology for the 2005 USGS assessment of undiscovered oil and gas resources, central North Slope, Alaska: U.S. Geological Survey Open-File Report 2005–1410, 82 p., also available online at *http://pubs.usgs.gov/of/2005/1410/.* (Accessed January 13, 2009.)

Shaw, Jerry, and Bachu, Stefan, 2002, Screening, evaluation, and ranking of oil reservoirs suitable for CO_2-flood EOR and carbon dioxide sequestration: Journal of Canadian Petroleum Technology, v. 41, no. 9, p. 51–61.

Skerlec, G.M., 1999, Evaluating top and fault seal, *in* Beaumont, E.A., and Foster, N.H., eds., Exploring for oil and gas traps, v. 3 *of* Treatise of petroleum geology; Handbook of petroleum geology: Tulsa, Okla., American Association of Petroleum Geologists, p. 10.3–10.94.

Spycher, Nicolas, and Pruess, Karsten, 2005, CO_2–H_2O mixtures in the geological sequestration of CO_2. II. Partitioning in chloride brines at 12–100°C and up to 600 bar: Geochimica et Cosmochimica Acta, v. 69, no. 13, p. 3309–3320, doi:10.1016/j.gca.2005.01.015.

Swanson, S.M., and Karlsen, A.W., 2009, USGS assessment of undiscovered oil and gas resources for the Oligocene Frio and Anahuac Formations, onshore Gulf of Mexico basin, USA [adapted from a poster presented at the American Association of Petroleum Geologists (AAPG) annual convention and exhibition, San Antonio, Tex., April 22, 2008]: Tulsa, Okla., AAPG Search and Discovery article 10178, 44 p., available only online at *http://www.searchanddiscovery.com/documents/2009/10178swanson/index.htm.* (Accessed March 3, 2009.)

Theis, C.V., 1935, The relation between the lowering of the piezometric surface and the rate and duration of discharge of a well using ground-water storage: American Geophysical Union Transactions, v. 16, p. 519–524.

U.S. Department of Energy, 2009, Carbon sequestration regional partnerships: U.S. Department of Energy Web page at *http://fossil.energy.gov/sequestration/partnerships/index.html.* (Accessed February 5, 2009.)

U.S. Department of Energy, National Energy Technology Laboratory, 2008a, Carbon sequestration atlas of the United States and Canada (2d ed.; Atlas II): 142 p., available online at *http://www.netl.doe.gov/technologies/carbon_seq/refshelf/atlasII/2008%20ATLAS_Introduction.pdf.*

U.S. Department of Energy, National Energy Technology Laboratory, 2008b, NatCarb—National carbon explorer: U.S. Department of Energy, National Energy Technology Laboratory, database at *http://www.natcarb.org/.* (Accessed February 9, 2009.)

U.S. Environmental Protection Agency, 2009, Safe Drinking Water Act (SDWA): Washington, D.C., U.S. Environmental Protection Agency Web site at *http://www.epa.gov/ogwdw/sdwa/index.html.* (Accessed January 14, 2009.)

U.S. Environmental Protection Agency, 2008, Federal requirements under the underground injection control (UIC) program for carbon dioxide (CO_2) geologic sequestration (GS) wells: Washington, D.C., U.S. Environmental Protection Agency, proposed rule, available online at *http://www.epa.gov/fedrgstr/EPA-WATER/2008/July/Day-25/w16626.htm.* (Accessed January 14, 2009.)

U.S. Geological Survey, 2009, GIS [files for the Frio Stable Shelf Oil and Gas Assessment Unit and the Frio Expanded Fault Zone Oil and Gas Assessment Unit], Gulf Coast assessments: U.S. Geological Survey Web site at *http://energy.er.usgs.gov/regional_studies/gulf_coast/gulf_coast_assessment.html.* (Accessed February 12, 2009.)

van der Meer, Bert, 1995, The CO_2 storage efficiency of aquifers: Energy Conversion and Management, v. 36, p. 513–518.

van der Meer, Bert, and Egberts, Paul, 2008, Calculating subsurface CO_2 storage capacities: The Leading Edge, v. 27, no. 4, p. 502–505, doi:10.1190/1.2907182. (Also available online at *http://tle.geoscienceworld.org/cgi/content/full/27/4/502.*) (Accessed January 14, 2009.)

Wallace, R.H., Kraemer, T.F., and Wesselman, J.B., 1981, Occurrence of geopressure in the northern Gulf of Mexico Basin: [Washington, D.C.,] U.S. Geological Survey, 1 map, scale 1:1,000,000.

Xu, Tianfu, Apps, J.A., and Pruess, Karsten, 2005, Mineral sequestration of carbon dioxide in a sandstone-shale system: Chemical Geology, v. 217, no. 3–4, p. 295–318, doi:10.1016/j.chemgeo.2004.12.015.

Glossary

barrels of oil equivalent (BOE)   A unit of petroleum volume in which the gas portion is expressed in terms of its energy equivalent in barrels of oil. For this assessment, 6,000 cubic feet of natural gas equals 1 barrel of oil equivalent (Klett and others, 2005b).

brine   Water having a salinity higher than that of average seawater, that is, more than 35,000 mg/L total dissolved solids (TDS).

buoyancy   Upward force on one phase (for example, a fluid) produced by the surrounding fluid (for example, a liquid or a gas) in which it is fully or partially immersed, caused by differences in density.

capillary force   Adhesive force that holds a fluid in a capillary or a pore space. Capillary force is a function of the properties of a fluid and surface and dimensions of the space. If the attraction between the fluid and surface is greater than the interaction of fluid molecules, the fluid will be held in place.

capillary pressure   In porous media containing two or more fluid phases, the difference in pressure between the wetting phase and the other phase(s) or between the other phases. The pressure difference results from surface tension at fluid interfaces and increases as the radius of curvature of the interfaces decreases. Capillary pressure is higher in rock with small pores and (or) small pore throats connecting pores than in rock with large pores and (or) large pore throats.

capillary trapping   The amount of CO_2 trapped within a pore that is not connected to a moving CO_2 plume. The CO_2 is held in place when the capillary forces on the CO_2 are greater than the buoyant forces of the CO_2 (Beaumont and Fiedler, 1999).

cap rock   *See* confining layer.

carbon capture and storage (CCS)   The process of capturing CO_2 from an emission source, (typically) converting it to a supercritical state, transporting it to an injection site, and injecting it into deep subsurface rock formations for long-term storage.

carbon dioxide plume   The extent underground, in three dimensions, of an injected carbon dioxide stream.

compartments   Permeable units that are isolated by permeability barriers from their surroundings. Extraction or injection of fluids in such units tends to cause pressure changes that persist for long periods of time because of the isolation.

conditional resource   Storage resource estimated for all physical traps (PTs) and saline formations (SFs) without taking the minimum size requirement into account.

confining layer   A geologic formation, group of formations, or part of a formation having lower permeability than the adjacent underlying or overlying formation; the difference in permeability causes preferential flow within the adjacent formation. Used synonymously with seal, aquitard, or aquiclude. The confining layer above a flow formation is commonly called a top seal.

C_{SE} *See* storage efficiency factor.

drive mechanism   Drive mechanism for the field indicates the injectivity of the storage space, particularly the role of water in the formation and the ability to replace it with CO_2. "Water drive" means that as hydrocarbons are withdrawn, hydrodynamic water flow replaces the volume of fluid withdrawn, providing pressure support for continued production. "Gas expansion" or "solution gas drive" means that the pressure is maintained by the compressibility of the gas phase. "Compaction" or "rock drive" means that pore space is destroyed during fluid production, which can lead to ground subsidence. Combinations of drive mechanisms are possible. Pressures measured in petroleum accumulations are equivalent to hydraulic head in aquifer systems.

ductility   Ability of a rock to sustain strain, under a given set of conditions, without losing strength or undergoing brittle failure (such as in fracturing or faulting). Shale, mudstone, and evaporites are typically considered to be very ductile, whereas crystalline rock, carbonate, and chert are considered to have low ductile strength within the expected temperature and pressure regime of CO_2 storage.

enhanced oil recovery (EOR)   Typically, the process of injecting a fluid (for example, water, brine, or CO_2) into an oil-bearing formation to recover residual oil. The injected fluid thins (decreases the viscosity) or displaces extractable oil, which is then available for recovery.

gas accumulation   A hydrocarbon accumulation composed primarily of gas, defined by the USGS as an accumulation having a gas:oil ratio of 20,000 cubic feet per barrel or greater.

gas:oil ratio (GOR)   Ratio of gas to oil (in cubic feet per barrel) in a hydrocarbon accumulation. GOR is calculated by using volumes of gas and oil at surface conditions.

geopressure (also overpressure)   Fluid pressure at depth that exceeds hydrostatic pressure (~0.43 to ~0.5 psi/ft).

geologic storage of CO_2   The long-term containment of carbon dioxide in subsurface geologic formations.

growth factor (C_G)   Determined by the assessor to represent the increase in resource that would result if the field area were extended to the spill point of the physical trap.

hydraulic conductivity (usually K)   Permeability multiplied by fluid density and gravity and divided by dynamic viscosity. It describes the resistance to flow offered by a porous medium to a particular liquid or gas. It is the proportionality constant in Darcy's law and has dimensions of length per unit time.

hydraulic diffusivity (usually κ)   The ratio of hydraulic conductivity K and specific storage. A quantity describing how quickly pressure or head perturbations propagate in porous media that is analogous to thermal diffusivity and chemical diffusivity. The value of κ will determine the magnitude and spreading of a pressure increase caused by fluid injection and the rate at which confining layers release or accept fluid.

hydraulic or fluid head (usually h)   A measure of the pressure and potential (or elevation) energy of a fluid and the level, above a measuring point, to which the fluid will rise in a standpipe or casing; normally used to characterize flow in systems without significant variations in fluid density, where flow is from high to low head (not from high to low pressure).

injectivity   The likelihood that CO_2 could enter a SAU, as defined by rock properties and subsurface pressure. It can also be thought of as the relative rate of injection by a single vertical well with a maximum pressure of 90 percent of the fracture gradient.

minimum depth of storage   To limit the potential of CO_2 migrating to pressure and temperature conditions where it could convert from the supercritical state to liquid and vapor. A minimum depth of storage of 3,000 ft is used in this CO_2 assessment methodology.

minimum storage size   The smallest storage size that is considered in the assessment process for physical traps (PTs). For this report, the minimum storage size for PTs is equivalent to 12,500,000 barrels, or approximately 2,000,000 cubic meters.

National Oil and Gas Assessment (NOGA)   U.S. Geological Survey National Oil and Gas Assessment, described at *http://energy.cr.usgs.gov/oilgas/noga/*.

net cumulative volume (NCV)   The sum of the cumulative volume of produced oil, gas, natural gas liquids, and water minus the total volume of injected gas and water.

net porous interval   Rock within the storage formation that is greater than a minimum porosity as determined by the assessment geologist.

oil accumulation   A hydrocarbon accumulation composed primarily of oil, defined by the USGS as an accumulation having an gas:oil ratio less than 20,000 cubic feet per barrel.

original oil in place (OOIP)   The volume of oil that was within a physical trap prior to the onset of production.

permeability   The capacity of a rock to transmit fluids, controlled by pore size and pore throat geometry.

physical trap (PT)   Conventional oil and gas traps that are available for potential CO_2 storage. PT_D refers to traps that were discovered during oil and gas exploration. PT_U refers to undiscovered physical traps, which are inferred from the volumes of technically recoverable, undiscovered oil and gas resources estimated by the USGS in NOGA reports.

porosity (Φ)   The part of a rock that is occupied by voids or pores. Pores can be connected by passages called pore throats, which allow for fluid flow, or pores can be isolated and inaccessible to fluid flow. Porosity is typically reported as a volume or percentage.

pressure gradient   The change in pore pressure per unit depth, typically in units of pounds per square inch per foot (psi/ft) or kilopascals per meter (kPa/m).

probability of containment   The probability that CO_2 will be contained within a physical trap or a saline formation. It is approximated from well density, well age, well seal technology utilized, evidence of surface seepage, presence and density of faults and other structural features, reactivity of the regional and local seal, and the seal's extent. The probability of containment is a number between 0 and 1, with a 1 being the certainty of containment within an individual physical trap or a saline formation.

reactivity   The propensity of minerals composing the rocks in a geologic formation to interact with formation water and injected carbon dioxide.

saline formations (SF)   The sedimentary rock layers that are saturated with formation water with total dissolved solids (TDS) greater than 10,000 mg/L TDS. In the CO_2 assessment methodology, the saline formation is composed of the remainder of the SAU not assessed by the PT methodology.

saline water   Water having salinities that are 10,000 to 35,000 mg/L total dissolved solids (TDS).

salinity   A measurement of the water properties determined by the total dissolved solids (TDS), generally reported in milligrams per liter.

seal   A geologic unit that inhibits the mixing or migration of fluids and gases between adjacent geologic units.

specific storage   Change in fluid volume per reference volume per change in fluid head. This quantity describes the ability of a porous medium to store and release fluid under changes in head (and thus pressure). It accounts for both fluid compression and matrix (or pore) deformation.

storage assessment unit (SAU)   A mappable volume of rock that includes a porous flow unit for CO_2 storage and confining layers.

storage efficiency factor (C_{SE})   Storage efficiency factor representing the fraction of the total available pore space that will be occupied by free-phase CO_2. C_{SE} values in the literature range from 0.01 to 0.05.

storage types for PTs (table 1):

 storage—EOR (S_{EOR})   Storage related to the net CO_2 left in place following CO_2 enhanced-oil-recovery practices. This storage is evaluated by method A in the physical trap assessment methodology.

 storage—net cumulative volume (S_{NCV})   The cumulative volume of fluid production (oil, gas, and water) minus the volume of fluid injected (water and gas). This storage is evaluated by method B in the physical trap assessment methodology.

 storage—total known volume (S_{TKV})   The total volume of pore space within the productive area of an oil and gas reservoir. This storage is evaluated by method C in the physical trap assessment methodology.

 storage—total trap volume (S_{TTV})   The resource volume of the PT to the spill point. This storage is evaluated by method D in the physical trap assessment methodology.

supercritical CO$_2$ Carbon dioxide is in a supercritical fluid state when both the temperature and pressure exceed the critical temperature of 31°C and pressure of 74 bars at which liquid and vapor CO$_2$ can no longer coexist.

technically accessible resource   The part of the total-in-place storage resource that may be available for CO$_2$ injection and storage estimated by using present-day geologic and hydrologic knowledge of the subsurface and engineering practice for CO$_2$ injection. Analogous to the term "technically recoverable resource" used in USGS oil and gas assessments.

total dissolved solids (TDS)   Synonymous with salinity; see salinity.

transmissivity (usually T)   The ability of a stratigraphic unit to accept or yield fluids with the properties included in hydraulic conductivity (K) of a stratigraphic unit multiplied by its thickness.

trapping   The physical and geochemical processes by which injected CO$_2$ is retained in the subsurface.

uncertainty of the mean   A distribution centered on the calculated mean of the raw data and bounded by values estimated by the assessment geologist to represent the possible range of mean values for the entire SF.

unconditional resource   Storage resource estimated for those physical traps and saline formations that meet the minimum size requirements.

Appendix A. Assessment Input Forms

A.1. Physical Traps (PTs) Assessment Model: Basic Input Data Form

The input sections for the physical trap form are described in text section 3.4.1.

PHYSICAL TRAPS (PTs) ASSESSMENT MODEL: BASIC INPUT DATA FORM

IDENTIFICATION INFORMATION

Assessment Geologist: _____ Date: _____
Region: _____ Number: _____
Province: _____ Number: _____
Storage Assessment Unit (SAU): _____ Number: _____
SAU Relationship to NOGA AU: _____
Based on Data as of: _____

Notes from Assessor: _____

CHARACTERISTICS OF THE STORAGE ASSESSMENT UNIT

1) Does the storage formation occur at depths between 3,000 and 13,000 ft?
   minimum: _____ mode: _____ maximum: _____
2) Area of storage formation at depths between 3,000 ft and 13,000 ft: _____
3) Is the storage formation overpressured (P/D> 0.5 psi/ft) at depths <13,000 ft? _____
   3a) If yes, area of SAU from 3,000 ft to known depth of overpressure: _____
4) Total Storage Formation Thickness (3,000-13,000 ft):
   minimum: _____ mode: _____ maximum: _____

NUMERICAL INPUTS

5) What is the minimum total capacity per Physical Trap (barrels)? _____
6) Number of discovered traps larger than the minimum size: _____
7) Based on the GOR < or > 20,000, the number of gas and oil PT_Ds.   a. Gas: _____
                                                                          b. Oil: _____

CHARACTERISTICS OF PT_Ds IN THE SAU

8) OOIP (BOE):   minimum: _____ median: _____ maximum: _____

9) Net Cum. Volume (barrels):   minimum: _____ median: _____ maximum: _____

10) Area (acres):   minimum: _____ median: _____ maximum: _____

11) Net Porous Interval (ft):   minimum: _____ mode: _____ maximum: _____

12) Porosity (fraction):   minimum: _____ mode: _____ maximum: _____

13) C_{SE} Factor: minimum: _____ mode: _____ maximum: _____

STORAGE VOLUME CALCULATION METHODS

A) Conventional EOR (S_{EOR}) = OOIP * I_R * C_{EOR}

14) Storage in PT_D (tons):   minimum: _____   median: _____   maximum: _____
From Line 8 and equation A.

15) Number of PT_Ds: _____
From Line 7b.

16) Storage in PT_U (tons):   minimum: _____   median: _____   maximum: _____
Calculated from internal analog, based on NOGA number and size results.

17) Number of PT_Us: minimum: _____   mode: _____   maximum: _____
Modified from NOGA results.

B) Net Cumulative Volume, NCV (S_{NCV}) = NCV * C_{WD} * C_{F1} * ρ_{CO2}

18) Storage in PT_D (tons):   minimum: _____   median: _____   maximum: _____
From Line 9.

19) Number of PT_Ds: _____
From Line 6.

20) Storage in PT_U (tons):   minimum: _____   median: _____   maximum: _____
Calculated from internal analog, based on NOGA number and size results.

21) Number of PT_Us: minimum: _____   mode: _____   maximum: _____
Modified from NOGA results.

C) Total Known Volume $(S_{TKV}) = T_A * T_I * N_{TP} * \Phi * C_{SE} * C_{F2} * \rho_{CO^2}$

22) Inputs for the assessment model PT_D probabilistic calculation:

Area (Line 10):	minimum: ____	median: ____	maximum: ____
Thickness (Line 11):	minimum: ____	mode: ____	maximum: ____
Porosity (Line 12):	minimum: ____	mode: ____	maximum: ____
C_{SE} Factor (Line 13):	minimum: ____	mode: ____	maximum: ____

23) Number of PT_Ds: ____
From Line 6.

24) Inputs for the assessment model PT_U probabilistic calculation:

Area (calculated):   minimum: ____   median: ____   maximum: ____
Calculated from internal analog, based on NOGA number and size results.

Thickness (Line 11):	minimum: ____	mode: ____	maximum: ____
Porosity (Line 12):	minimum: ____	mode: ____	maximum: ____
C_{SE} Factor (Line 13):	minimum: ____	mode: ____	maximum: ____

25) Number of PT_Us: minimum: ____   mode: ____   maximum: ____
Modified from NOGA results.

D) Total Trap Volume to spill point $(S_{TTV}) = S_{TKV} * C_G$

26) Same inputs as Line 22 S_{TKV}, with addition of Growth Factor (C_G).
Growth Factor (C_G):   ____

27) Number of PT_Ds: ____
From Line 6.

28) Same inputs as Line 24 PT_U S_{TKV}, with addition of Growth Factor (C_G).
Growth Factor (C_G):   ____

29) Number of PT_Us: minimum: ____   mode: ____   maximum: ____
Modified from NOGA results.

PHYSICAL TRAP PROBABILITY OF CONTAINMENT

Probability of occurrence (0-1.0)

30) Probability of Containment:
     See text for description and determination.
                                   _____

SELECTED ANCILLARY DATA

Assessor is expected to separately describe physical, chemical, and mineralogical characterisitcs of the reservoir and confining layers that may influence (marked "yes" below) CO_2 sequestration capability.

	Yes	No	Not Applicable
Injectivity:	_____	_____	_____
Depth to Top of Storage:	_____	_____	_____
Confining Layer Characteristics:	_____	_____	_____
Natural Seismic Risk:	_____	_____	_____
Reservoir Architecture:	_____	_____	_____
Drive Mechanism:	_____	_____	_____
Reactivity:	_____	_____	_____
Geologic Age:	_____	_____	_____
Extent of Diagenesis:	_____	_____	_____
Formation Water Composition:	_____	_____	_____
Mineral Composition:	_____	_____	_____
CO_2-Brine-Mineral Interactions at T and P:	_____	_____	_____
Formation Water Salinity:	_____	_____	_____

ALLOCATIONS OF PTs TO STATES
Surface Allocations (uncertainty of a fixed value)

1 _____ represents _____ area % of the SAU

   Volume % in entity   mode: _____

2 _____ represents _____ area % of the SAU

   Volume % in entity   mode: _____

3 _____ represents _____ area % of the SAU

   Volume % in entity   mode: _____

4 _____ represents _____ area % of the SAU

   Volume % in entity   mode: _____

5 _____ represents _____ area % of the SAU

   Volume % in entity   mode: _____

6 _____ represents _____ area % of the SAU

   Volume % in entity   mode: _____

7 _____ represents _____ area % of the SAU

   Volume % in entity   mode: _____

8 _____ represents _____ area % of the SAU

   Volume % in entity   mode: _____

ALLOCATIONS OF PTs TO GENERAL LAND OWNERSHIPS
Surface Allocations (uncertainty of a fixed value)

1   Federal Lands _____ represents _____ area % of the SAU

       Volume % in entity   mode: _____

2   Private Lands _____ represents _____ area % of the SAU

       Volume % in entity   mode: _____

3   Tribal Lands _____ represents _____ area % of the SAU

       Volume % in entity   mode: _____

4   Other Lands _____ represents _____ area % of the SAU

       Volume % in entity   mode: _____

5   State 1 Lands _____ represents _____ area % of the SAU

       Volume % in entity   mode: _____

6   _____ represents _____ area % of the SAU

       Volume % in entity   mode: _____

7   _____ represents _____ area % of the SAU

       Volume % in entity   mode: _____

8   _____ represents _____ area % of the SAU

       Volume % in entity   mode: _____

ALLOCATIONS OF PTs TO CRITICAL LAND AREAS
Surface Allocations (uncertainty of a fixed value, does not total 100%)

1 Offshore Storage _____ represents _____ area % of the SAU

   Volume % in entity   minimum   mode   maximum
                           _____   _____   _____

2 Urban Lands _____ represents _____ area % of the SAU

   Volume % in entity   minimum   mode   maximum
                           _____   _____   _____

3 _____ represents _____ area % of the SAU

   Volume % in entity   minimum   mode   maximum
                           _____   _____   _____

ALLOCATIONS OF PTs TO PROVINCES
Surface Allocations (uncertainty of a fixed value)

1 _____ represents _____ area % of the SAU

   Volume % in entity   mode: _____

2 _____ represents _____ area % of the SAU

   Volume % in entity   mode: _____

3 _____ represents _____ area % of the SAU

   Volume % in entity   mode: _____

4 _____ represents _____ area % of the SAU

   Volume % in entity   mode: _____

74

A.2. Saline Formation (SF) Assessment Model: Basic Input Data Form

The input sections for the saline formation form are described in text section 3.4.2.

SALINE FORMATION (SF) ASSESSMENT MODEL: BASIC INPUT DATA FORM

IDENTIFICATION INFORMATION

Assessment Geologist: _____ Date: _____

Region: _____ Number: _____

Province: _____ Number: _____

Storage Assessment Unit (SAU): _____ Number: _____

SAU Relationship to NOGA AU: _____

Based on Data as of: _____

Notes from Assessor: _____

_____

CHARACTERISTICS OF THE STORAGE ASSESSMENT UNIT

1) Does the storage formation occur at depths between 3,000 and 13,000 ft?

        minimum: _____ mode: _____ maximum: _____

2) Area of storage formation at depths between 3,000 ft and 13,000 ft:

3) Is the storage formation overpressured (P/D> 0.5 psi/ft) at depths <13,000 ft?

        3a) If yes, area of SAU from 3,000 ft to known depth of overpressure:

4) Total Storage Formation Thickness (3,000-13,000 ft):

        minimum: _____ mode: _____ maximum: _____

AREA OF THE SALINE FORMATION CALCULATION

5) What is the sum of areas of all PTs larger than the minimum size (acres)? _____

6) What is the sum of the areas for all undiscovered PTs larger than the minimum size?

        minimum: _____ mode: _____ maximum: _____

Area of Saline Formation Equation

Asf = Asau - (Aptd+Aptu)

where
Asf = Area of Saline Formation
Asau = Area of Storage Assessment Unit (Line 2 or 3a if overpressured)
Aptd = Area of Physical Traps (fixed value from Line 5)
Aptu = Area of Undiscovered Traps (distribution from Line 6)

7) Area of Saline Formation (acres):

        minimum: _____ mean: _____ maximum: _____

CHARACTERISTICS OF THE SALINE FORMATION

8) Net Porous Interval (ft):   minimum: _____   mean: _____   maximum: _____

9) Porosity (fraction):   minimum: _____   mean: _____   maximum: _____

10) C_{SE} Factor: minimum: _____   mode: _____   maximum: _____

SALINE FORMATION STORAGE VOLUME

SF Storage Volume = $T_A * T_I * \Phi * C_{SE}$

11) Inputs for the assessment model probabilistic calculation:
Inputs include the mean, from the raw data, and lower and upper uncertainties of the mean value.
Uncertainties of the mean values are chosen by the assessing geologist. See text for further explanation.

Area: mean (Line 7): _____   lower uncertainty of the mean: _____
                                        upper uncertainty of the mean: _____

Thickness: mean (Line 8): _____   lower uncertainty of the mean: _____
                                            upper uncertainty of the mean: _____

Porosity: mean (Line 9): _____   lower uncertainty of the mean: _____
                                           upper uncertainty of the mean: _____

C_{SE} Factor (Line 10):   minimum: _____   mode: _____   maximum: _____

SALINE FORMATION PROBABILITY OF CONTAINMENT

Probability of occurrence (0-1.0)

12) Probability of Containment: _____
         See text for description and determination.

SELECTED ANCILLARY DATA

Assessor is expected to separately describe physical, chemical, and mineralogical characterisitcs of the reservoir and confining layers that may influence (marked "yes" below) CO_2 sequestration capability.

	Yes	No	Not Applicable
Injectivity:	_____	_____	_____
Depth to Top of Storage:	_____	_____	_____
Confining Layer Characteristics:	_____	_____	_____
Natural Seismic Risk:	_____	_____	_____
Reservoir Architecture:	_____	_____	_____
Drive Mechanism:	_____	_____	_____
Reactivity:	_____	_____	_____
Geologic Age:	_____	_____	_____
Extent of Diagenesis:	_____	_____	_____
Formation Water Composition:	_____	_____	_____
Mineral Composition:	_____	_____	_____
CO_2-Brine-Mineral Interactions at T and P:	_____	_____	_____
Formation Water Salinity:	_____	_____	_____

ALLOCATIONS OF THE SF TO STATES
Surface Allocations (uncertainty of a fixed value)

1 _____ represents _____ area % of the SAU

    Volume % in entity   mode: _____

2 _____ represents _____ area % of the SAU

    Volume % in entity   mode: _____

3 _____ represents _____ area % of the SAU

    Volume % in entity   mode: _____

4 _____ represents _____ area % of the SAU

    Volume % in entity   mode: _____

5 _____ represents _____ area % of the SAU

    Volume % in entity   mode: _____

6 _____ represents _____ area % of the SAU

    Volume % in entity   mode: _____

7 _____ represents _____ area % of the SAU

    Volume % in entity   mode: _____

8 _____ represents _____ area % of the SAU

    Volume % in entity   mode: _____

ALLOCATIONS OF THE SF TO GENERAL LAND OWNERSHIPS
Surface Allocations (uncertainty of a fixed value)

1 Federal Lands _____ represents _____ area % of the SAU

   Volume % in entity   mode: _____

2 Private Lands _____ represents _____ area % of the SAU

   Volume % in entity   mode: _____

3 Tribal Lands _____ represents _____ area % of the SAU

   Volume % in entity   mode: _____

4 Other Lands _____ represents _____ area % of the SAU

   Volume % in entity   mode: _____

5 State 1 Lands _____ represents _____ area % of the SAU

   Volume % in entity   mode: _____

6 _____ represents _____ area % of the SAU

   Volume % in entity   mode: _____

7 _____ represents _____ area % of the SAU

   Volume % in entity   mode: _____

8 _____ represents _____ area % of the SAU

   Volume % in entity   mode: _____

ALLOCATIONS OF THE SF TO CRITICAL LAND AREAS
Surface Allocations (uncertainty of a fixed value, does not total 100%)

1   Offshore Storage _____ represents _____ area % of the SAU

    Volume % in entity   minimum   mode   maximum

                           _____   _____   _____

2   Urban Lands _____ represents _____ area % of the SAU

    Volume % in entity   minimum   mode   maximum

                           _____   _____   _____

3   _____ represents _____ area % of the SAU

    Volume % in entity   minimum   mode   maximum

                           _____   _____   _____

ALLOCATIONS OF THE SF TO PROVINCES
Surface Allocations (uncertainty of a fixed value)

1   _____ represents _____ area % of the SAU

    Volume % in entity   mode: _____

2   _____ represents _____ area % of the SAU

    Volume % in entity   mode: _____

3   _____ represents _____ area % of the SAU

    Volume % in entity   mode: _____

4   _____ represents _____ area % of the SAU

    Volume % in entity   mode: _____